Unpublished Romance

THE FORCE OF LIFE

Zibia Gasparetto

Romance dictated by Spirit
LUCIUS

Translation to English:
Carmen Carrasco Martinez
Lima, Perú, July 2021

Original Title in Portuguese:

"A Força da Vida"

© Zibia Gasparetto, 2019

Revision:

Beatriz Rueda Stella, Campinas, Brazil

Houston, Texas, USA

E–mail: contact@worldspiritistinstitute.org

About the Medium

Zibia Gasparetto is a Brazilian spiritual writer. She was born in Campinas. She is married to Aldo Luis Gasparetto and has four children. According to her story, a night in 1950 she woke up and began to walk around the house speaking German, a language that she didn't know. The next day, her husband bought a book about Spiritism to study together.

Her husband assists the spiritual association Federação Espírita do Estado de São Paulo, but she has to stay at home. On one occasion, Gasparetto felt a severe pain in her arm which it begins to move around without control. After Aldo gives her a pencil and paper, she begins to write quickly. Writing her first novel "And Love Won" signed by a spirit called Lucius. The manuscript was typed. Gasparetto showed a Historian professor of São Paulo University, who was interested in Spiritism too. Two weeks later, she receives the confirmation that her book will be published by LAKE Editorial. In her late years, Gasparetto used her computer four times a week to write stories dictated by her spirits.

She wrote usually at night for one or two hours. "They [Spirits] are not available, to work many days per week", she explains. "I don't know why, but each one of them just appears once a week. I try to change but I couldn't" As a result, she used to have one night a week, which each spirit communicated with her.

See the last available books of Zibia Gasparetto translated in English at the end of this book.

Contents

PROLOGUE..6
CHAPTER 1..14
CHAPTER 2..34
CHAPTER 3..51
CHAPTER 4..65
CHAPTER 5..80
CHAPTER 6..93
CHAPTER 7..111
CHAPTER 8..124
CHAPTER 9..138
CHAPTER 10..155
CHAPTER 11..166
CHAPTER 12..174
CHAPTER 13..178
CHAPTER 14..190
CHAPTER 15..198
CHAPTER 16..210
CHAPTER 17..240
CHAPTER 18..258
CHAPTER 19..280
EPILOGUE...289

PROLOGUE

It was dawn when the caravan stopped in front of the gate of the Campos da Paz colony. The chief took the lead and placed his hand on the lock, from where a golden light was coming out. The door then opened softly, and they entered in silence. There were, between them, nine people, and six of them were carrying a stretcher on which was a wounded man, his face swollen, pale, looking dead.

– Take him to the emergency area. He needs to be settled. After I talk to Jules, I will go to see him – explained Jose'.

The first rays of the morning were beginning to appear, and he walked quickly to the immense property located in the middle of a magnificent garden, entering immediately through the main door.

The movement was great, and several busy people were circulating the hall. Joseph made his way to a corridor where there were several rooms and stopped in front of one of them. The door opened, and a tall, dark man, who appeared to be about 50 years old and dressed in a white vest, approached, staring at him with shining eyes. With some anxiety Jules asked:

– So, then, José did you get it?

– Yes. I managed to bring him in, but he is in terrible shape. They took him to the recovery room in isolation.

– I knew it wasn't going to be easy. Bringing him in was a victory. Let's go over there, because I want to see him.

The two men went to the garden and walked to the other side of the wall, where there were some individual living quarters. One of the men in the group would watch the door, and they would make their way there.

Passing through the door, they went through a small room and into a chamber illuminated by a blue light. There were various devices operating with the colored lights. Some were thin and transparent, and different colored liquids were moving them.

A middle-aged woman with an attentive physiognomy and bright eyes accompanied the work of the two nurses, who were carefully assessing the case, taking notes on a chart.

Jules approached the bed with interest, embraced the woman with affection and said with emotion:

– How good to see you, Norma!

– I couldn't help but come. Olavo is in my heart.

Jules approached the patient, who had not yet regained consciousness, and fixed his injured face. He then placed his right hand on the forehead of the patient for a few seconds, went down to the heart and then, looking at Norma, commented:

– Thank goodness he is here. That gives us hope that he can get better.

– Yes, when, years ago that tragedy happened– which I tried so hard to avoid– I promised myself that I would do everything so that they could forgive each other, understand and get back on the road to progress.

Many years passed, and he rolled further and further into the abyss until he became insensitive and cruel. However, now, I feel that he is in a position to become sensitive, to become aware of the truth and to take control of his own life.

– I have waited for this time, vibrating so that he reacts and manages to become aware of things, recovering the joy of living. The moment is propitious, because everything is in his favor. If he manages to get ahead, he will certainly get everything he wants to be happy.

– I feel he will get in. Renata also desires his well–being, and the others vibrate for him. And, even if she does not comment on it, I believe that the love she felt for this man is still alive.

– Well, I feel a tightness in my chest just thinking about that possibility. Renata is doing well now, she has regained the joy of living, and she is making plans for her happiness. I would not like them to get back together

Norma smiled slightly and replied:

– Thus speaks your father's heart, Jules, however, I think that, in those ashes, there is still a hidden ember, and one day everything will return to the scene. Every life is an opportunity to evolve, and when it strives, the spirit has better conditions to realize more.

– I am not speaking as a parent, Norma. I know that kinship only works when we are in the world, and we have long since left earth. I speak as a person, evaluating that both are opposite spirits.

– Sometimes, opposites meet so that both can learn. However, this is only a hypothesis that may never happen. We do not know the fate that awaits them.

– Did you come to stay, Norma? – Jules asked.

– I don't have much time, as I have other commitments, but at least I will stay here for a day or two – the woman clarified.

– It would be a great pleasure to have you in my home during that time – Jules said sincerely.

– Thank you very much, but Olivia already invited me, and I accepted. I promise we will be together if possible.

– I need to go, but I'll keep an eye on the case. When he wakes up, let me know.

Jules said goodbye and left. Norma looked at Olavo's traumatized face, placed her hand on his forehead and began to pray.

Colored energies came out of her hands and penetrated the forehead of the sick man, running through his body, which shuddered from time to time.

The nurses had already taken care of the patient's hygiene and wounds and had dressed him in a white robe. Under the effect of the treatment of the colored lights, which ran through the centers of strength, Olavo's body was illuminated.

Little by little, his physiognomy became more relaxed, serene, and his breathing became calmer. Norma smiles with satisfaction. The patient was improving, and she waited anxiously for him to wake up. Olavo, despite everything, continued to sleep, however, with more serenity.

Time passed, and Norma continued to watch over Olavo at the bedside. In the late afternoon, when Jules returned, she only said:

– He still sleeps, but I think that sleep is part of the treatment. The more Olavo rests, receives more regenerative energies, and thinks about nothing, the faster he will accept the situation and suffer less.

Jules placed his hand on Olavo's chest for a few seconds and then answered:

– I hope so. From the last time we met him, we did not manage to make him accept the treatment.

– I feel that this time it will be different, Jules. He got to the bottom of the well. Remember that it was Olavo who asked for help.

– Let's believe in the best, in the end, at some point he will have to give in. You've already spent the whole day by his side. Go get some rest. I'll just sit here and if he wakes up, I'll let you know.

Norma got up and said:

– Okay. I think Renata is sensing his presence and needs me. Norma hurried out, walked across the garden and, before reaching the building, met Renata coming the other way. Seeing Norma, the young woman approached her, saying in distress:

– I want to see him, Norma! I feel that Olavo is in a very bad way. I need to help him somehow.

– Calm down, Renata. Everything is fine. He received treatment and now, he is sleeping peacefully. When he wakes up, Olavo will be much better.

– I feel uneasy. I need to see him.

– I felt your agony and came to stay with you. Jules is with him. So Olavo woke up, he promised to let us know. Calm down. Let's go home.

Renata held Norma's hands tightly and, looking into her eyes, asked:

– Are you sure he won't run away again? I'm afraid he'll come after Antonio again.

– He's not strong enough to get out here. Besides that, he doesn't know where Antonio is. Let's go home.

– I want to see him. Assess the situation closely.

– Your presence may bring unpleasant memories to the surface, so forgetting the past is often a relief. Calm your heart. Everything is under control.

Tears streamed down Renata's face, and she said emotionally:

– But I want to help, in the end, I was the cause of the misunderstanding between them. I need to do something to erase that guilt that is bothering me. I asked for him to be brought here so that I could intervene in some way and put an end to this hatred that has caused us so much unhappiness.

– Everything has its moment. Your intention is good, but the time has not yet come for you to interfere. Take care of yourself, improve your life, study, learn, work for your well-being and, one day, when you are better, maybe you will be able to do what you intend to do. Let's go. It was getting dark, the stars were twinkling in the sky, and the moon was brightening the night. Norma hugged Renata, who laid her head on her friend's chest letting herself go. The two of them rose, leaving the place and, soon after, they approached the earth's crust, in a neighborhood of Rio de Janeiro. They stopped in front of a sophisticated house, located in a tree-lined street and went down, crossing the roof of the room where Renata is asleep.

Delicately, Norma placed her back on the body. Renata shuddered, and Norma stretched out her hands over the young woman saying in a calm voice:

– Rest, my dear! Don't be afraid and trust in God! We are with you, and everything will be alright.

Renata rocked on the bed, turned on her side and continued sleeping. A woman entered the room and seeing Norma asked:

– And, so, did everything go well?

– Yes Margarida. He is already being treated and, this time, I think we will succeed. Take good care of our little girl. She is very nervous, feeling the events. If you need anything, let me know.

– You can rest assured. I'll be attentive.

– I need to go now. God bless you," Norma said goodbye.

The women embraced and then Norma rose, crossed the ceiling and disappeared into the heights.

Margarida sat on the side of the bed and stroked Renata's forehead, who was still asleep.

– We will take care of you. Nothing bad will happen to you. Margarita had taken care of Renata practically since her birth, whom she loved very much. Sensitive and kind, the woman had been in contact with the spirits of light since her early childhood, that is why she perceived Norma's presence and from her she perceived information about Renata's past, which made her offer to collaborate.

Margarida did not know well that she would see, but she felt that the time would come when her little girl would need her, and she was willing to help.

Noticing that, still asleep, Renata shivered from time to time, Maria sat down next to the young girl's bed and kept her hand on her forehead. Soon after, she began to pray, asking for help from spiritual friends.

CHAPTER 1

The doorbell rang, and Margarita went to open the door. In front of her a young man held a box lined with gold paper with a white flower on top.

– Delivery of Sedalinda for Miss Renata Albuquerque.

– You may deliver.

– Please sign the receipt.

Margarida signed and the delivery man left. With a smile on her face, she walked up the stairs carrying the box, stopped in front of the door and knocked softly, saying:

–Your package has arrived:

– Your order arrived, may I come in?

Immediately, Renata opened the door and joyfully grabbed the package, placing it on the bed. Tall and with a shapely body, the young woman had dark hair, which contrasted with her fair skin and green eyes. With full lips, she was in the prime of her 22 years.

Margarida watched Renata with sparkling eyes, admiring the young woman's elegant gestures and haughty attitude. She had started working in the house as a nanny when Renata was only two years old, and she was a child at first sight.

Renata was the daughter of Dionísio Albuquerque, a very successful criminal lawyer famous for his oratory, which placed him among the best in the field, and of Dona Eunice de Lima Albuquerque, an intelligent woman who, although she did not work outside the home, accompanied her husband's cases. In all of them, Dionísio always exchanged ideas with the wife, taking her arguments into consideration. Paulo José was 25 years old, and the boy's father wanted him to study law, but he had no intention of following this advice.

Paulo José did not appreciate reading, but he liked the arts. He liked music and the night. He was on par with the artistic movement of the city, was a television enthusiast and a great admirer of beautiful women who circulated around him. Rich, attractive, well-to-do, Paulo José was always ready to have fun, surrounded by beautiful girls and cheerful friends.

At his parents' insistence, he enrolled in the Faculty of Fine Arts. He tried to dedicate himself to painting but was unable to continue; to the study of the piano – he tried for more than a year, but gave up –; and, finally, he decided that he would dedicate himself to a career as an actor. Paulo José then enrolled in a theater school on the recommendation of some friends and began to obtain his first results.

Paulo José's parents did not look favorably on this situation, as they would like the young man to choose a profession that would give him a more promising future. However, when he obtained his first successes, he continued to insist on this path. He dreamed of becoming a great actor.

Renata, in turn, was the opposite of her brother. An inveterate reader since childhood, she graduated in Literature and nurtured the dream of becoming a writer. Although she liked to dance, she was very introspective and preferred quiet places, where she could enjoy her inner world and understand a little more about life and its mysteries.

On that Saturday, Renata's parents were throwing a party at a crowded club in the city to celebrate their thirtieth wedding anniversary.

In front of Margarita's shining eyes, who followed Renata's every gesture, the young woman took the dress out of the box and spread it on the bed. The employee's heart began to beat faster, and she did not hold back:

– How beautiful, Renata, I've never seen a dress like that! That shade of green will match your eyes! You're going to look stunning!

– It's really very pretty.

– Mrs. Eunice set the time at the beauty parlor and asked you not to be late.

– I would prefer to do my own thing, my own way. I don't feel like going to the salon.

– Your mother will be upset with you.

Renata shrugged her shoulders:

– Nonsense. She can go, do as she likes, but I want to feel good, to go to the party the way I like it. I don't want to look like a salon doll. Have you noticed how they all do everything the same? They always wear the latest hairstyle, the dresses in the colors of the moment? Even the way they walk is copied from movie artists! And I am what I am. I want to be what I am, true. Why dress up to look like everyone else when I can be myself?

– You must get ready, Renata. Your mother intends to leave in half an hour.

– Margarida, let my mother know that I've decided not to go to the salon.

The maid hesitated, and Renata insisted:

– Go on, quickly, go! Didn't you hear what I said?

Margarida went out pale, and Renata stood in front of the mirror thinking how she would like to fix her hair.

A short time later, Eunice entered her daughter's room, saying irritated:

– Are you still not ready? Renata, we can't be late! We're overdue.

The young woman answered in a calm voice:

– Margarida didn't give you the message?

– She gave it to me, but I pretended not to listen. You're going to the salon anyway, even if I must drag you there.

– You're forcing the issue. I don't want to go!

Eunice shot her with her eyes.

– But you will go.

– Why do you think I need to look like the other girls? To look like the other girls? You yourself keep saying that they look like dolls! That they don't possess any naturalness.

Do you want me to be like them? Well, I refuse, mother, I have the right to dress up as I please!

Dionísio appeared at the door, exclaiming:

– What's going on here, why are they talking so loudly?

Irritated, Eunice fixed her husband, and Renata argued:

– Mom wants to force me to go to the beauty salon, comb my hair and be made up like all the other young girls, and I want to do it my own way.

Dionísio looked at Eunice, shook his head and said in a calm voice:

– You go. Let her do as she wants. Renata always presented herself very well, and I'm sure she will look as always.

Eunice took a deep breath, looked back and forth, then said in a threatening voice:

– On this night, I want everything to be perfect! If you don't look as I want, I will be very sad.

Renata ran to her mother's side, hugged her and said in a loving voice:

– Thank you for understanding, mom. In your tribute, I'm going to do my best, you'll love it!

Dionísio secured his wife's arm:

– Come on, Eunice, you can't be late. The two of us need to arrive first to receive the guests.

– I asked Paulo José to arrive earlier to check that everything is as we agreed.

– In that case, everything will be fine.

Dionísio and Eunice left, and Renata breathed a sigh of relief. It was still early, and she settled into an armchair, put her feet up on a stool, picked up a book and began to read.

Perhaps because the afternoon was dying, the sun was setting and the thin curtains were closed, barely moved by the light breeze coming through the window, Renata felt relaxed. Surrendered to that atmosphere of tranquility and peace, the young woman let the book she was reading slip from her hands until, at last, she fell asleep.

Once she fell asleep, Renata dreamed that she was in a beautiful garden, full of flowers of various sizes and colors, where she walked with confidence. Intimately, she felt that she knew that place. Suddenly, she saw a woman sitting on a bench, approaching, she greeted the woman happily:

– Norma! It's good to see you!

The two women embraced each other warmly, sat down and suddenly Renata remembered something. With a serious look on her face, she asked:

– And, so, he's awake already?

– Yes, he's all right. He accepted the treatment and asked to stay.

Renata breathed a sigh of relief.

– That's good. I hope he doesn't have any relapses.

– Jules is taking care of him, this time, without arguing. They understood each other, which was already a big step. Now everything is in favor of understanding.

– I am afraid that he will want to reincarnate. I prefer that he continue under the care of our superiors. It is more guaranteed.

– Don't worry. You know that he will only reincarnate again when he is able to take advantage of the opportunity. All this is well planned. Life is not moralistic, it is functional. Things only work out well, when the spirit discovers how the laws of the universe work. The laws that govern our life on Earth.

Renata sighed, thought a little and then said:

– I know. Forgive me. It's just that somehow, I have a feeling that I will have to be part of that situation and I feel a little afraid.

– Today, everything is different. Take away that fear, for it will only make you weaker. Your strength is in the belief that everything will happen at the right time and that the circumstances will be all favorable. Do not forget that.

Someone knocked on the bedroom door, Renata woke up and looked around, not knowing where she was.

Margarida entered the room and said:

– Didn't you manage to get ready yet? Your mother is here, she's getting dressed and wants to leave in half an hour. You need to hurry, Renata!

The young woman got up in a hurry:

– Set everything aside for me. I'm going to take a quick bath.

As she let the water run down her body, Renata thought about the dream she had just had. The young woman remembered walking through a beautiful garden and talking with a woman who was very dear to her. Everything happened naturally, but Renata could not remember what they had talked about. Who was that woman? Where did she know her from? She wondered but could not find any answers.

Renata believed that it was all just a dream, but the memory of the encounter remained strong in her heart, as if it had really happened. That encounter seemed all too real to her, and she carried that feeling within her for a long time.

While the young woman was getting ready for the party and putting on her make-up, fragments of the dream she had reappeared in her memory, and Renata struggled to keep her attention on what she was doing. When she finally got ready, the young woman went down to the living room and breathed a sigh of relief when she noticed that Eunice was not yet downstairs. Renata then took the opportunity to check her appearance in the large mirror in the hall and liked what she saw.

The dark green dress of pure silk fit her body like a glove. The neckline exposed Renata's shapely white neck.

Her eyes looked like two emeralds, and the dark hair, slightly wavy, was whimsically held in place and molded the young woman's face, giving her the appearance of a goddess.

Accompanied by her husband, Eunice descended the stairs and approached her daughter, fixing her eyes on the young woman for a few seconds. Soon after, the matriarch's face relaxed, and she commented:

– You look very pretty! – Eunice said with satisfaction.

– Didn't I tell you she knew what she wanted? – Dionísio commented provocatively.

– Congratulations, daughter! You look like a fairy!

– Thank you, mom! And you look wonderful, and daddy is, as always, very elegant.

Eunice ordered:

– Let's get going. I don't want to be late.

It was the end of summer, and the night was beautiful. During the drive, while the couple talked about the party, Renata thought about the dream she had during the afternoon and tried hard to remember the conversation she had with that woman. Why was she so worried in the dream? She felt that there was something important, but no matter how hard she tried, she could not remember the details.

Passing through the gate and through the gardens of the club, the car stopped at the social entrance of the party room. Dionísio, Eunice and Renata, then, got out of the car and walked to the place where the party would take place.

In the hall, the lighted lights reflected the brightness of the crystals, and there were flowers artistically distributed and positioned on all sides. The tables, neatly arranged for dinner, were arranged around the dance floor. In a corner, the musicians, in gala costumes, were seated on the stage and were already preparing to play.

Paulo José approached the parents, accompanied by the organizer of the party, who bowed in front of the couple and said:

– I hope everything is to your liking.

Eunice looked at Paulo José as if asking the son for details, who, noticing the hand gesture, said:

– Everything is fine, mom! This party will be unforgettable! Everyone will love it! Everything is nice and well done.

– Your dad and I are going to receive the people, so I ask you to be attentive to everything so that nothing is missing for the guests and so that everyone is satisfied.

– Everything is under control; I am in charge. You must celebrate, seize the moment. Enjoy yourselves.

The orchestra began to play and then the guests began to arrive. Soon after, a cocktail began to be served.

The young women surrounded Paulo José and the boy's friends, and the conversation in the group began to get lively. Renata tried her best to be polite to everyone but tried to detach herself as best she could from the people. She didn't want to talk to anyone. She preferred to observe the beauty of the environment, the flowers and the faces of the people. She tried to imagine what was behind the social mask they wore and what, in fact, mattered to them. I didn't do that out of curiosity, but to understand more about life, everyone's feelings, people's dreams and their desires for happiness. When I had a conversation with someone, it was always for that purpose.

The orchestra was good, and the party was lively. The young men hung around Renata, vying for her attention. In the end, the young woman was especially beautiful that night, in her dark green silk dress, which looked more like a delicate extension of her eyes. Even if she moved shyly around the room, the young woman's beauty was an eye-catcher.

In addition to a great passion for books, Renata loved to dance. However, she did not like to linger and chat while dancing. She preferred to feel the music, to get into its rhythm. Almost always the young men who asked her to dance had the objective of wooing her, but Renata, in turn, politely avoided them, thus losing the pleasure of continuing.

At a certain point, already a little tired, Renata decided to walk through the garden and take advantage of the evening breeze. The young woman then looked for a discreet bench and sat down. The night was clear, and the full moon reigned amidst the stars with its silver light.

The beauty of the moment touched the soul of the young woman, who felt an immense nostalgia for something that she certainly could not define. Renata, then, began to wonder where that emotion came from and how it was possible to feel nostalgia for something indefinable.

Renata closed her eyes and the image of a beautiful place full of flowers came to her mind. The scene was so vivid that the young woman felt a delicate perfume invading her nose. When Renata wanted to look for more details of that scene that was drawn in strong colors in her mind, everything suddenly disappeared, and she could not pick it up again. However, the image was so strong that it remained engraved in her memory. An energy of well-being then invaded the young woman, who again began to question herself: "Where have I seen that place? Where is the moon so bright like that? Where the blue is more vivid, and the energies are lighter and more pleasant? I'm sure I've been to that place before. But when?"

At that moment, disturbed voices brought her back to reality. A couple was arguing very close to where Renata was. The young woman came to think about leaving, but then imagined that, if she did, it might inhibit them. She thought it best to stand still and wait for them to leave.

– You can't do that with me! What am I going to do with my life now? You must marry me! If my dad finds out, you won't get out of this story alive!

– I never promised you anything and I'm not going to marry you. I can't, you know that. I have no conditions to marry you now! You gave yourself because you wanted to. I never forced you.

– You never forced me, but you accepted my love, and now you want to get rid of the body! Watch out, I'm desperate! You don't know what I'm capable of. Besides, you don't know what a desperate woman is capable of!

– I'm not afraid of your father or your threats. Your attitude is suspicious. You did that on purpose. I don't even know if that son is mine.

– You're a commoner! I'll go into that room right now and tell you all about it. I'll make a scandal! I want to see where your reputation as a good person is going to end!

The young woman said this shouting, and then she walked away with quick steps. With bated breath, Renata strained her ears and waited for the man's footsteps to move away. The unpleasant scene left her indisposed, not only because of the affair, but also because of the fear that the young woman would do what she promised. It was her parents' party, and a scandal would be disastrous.

However, the man did not move, and Renata did not want to be seen. Carefully and quietly, the young woman moved some branches away from the bush trying to see who it was. He was still sitting on the bench, but with his back turned. He was tall, elegant, had dark hair and an athletic bearing. Resigned, Renata waited for him to come out.

Half an hour later, she heard the man's footsteps and, from the direction he was heading, concluded that he was returning to the living room. Renata took a deep breath and returned to the party, looking around, trying to find out if the young woman with whom the man had argued would do what he had promised. Everything, however, continued to be calm and the party was carefree and cheerful. Renata made her way to the parents' table, who were talking with two friends.

Estela, daughter of a couple of friends, approached Renata and asked:

– Where were you? The boys didn't give me any peace of mind trying to find out about you.

– I didn't want to dance with them, Estela?

– I can't understand you! I would like to have your luck, to always be surrounded by suitors. I don't understand you; you love to dance.

– For the pleasure of enjoying the dance, Estela. But they want to make me fall in love, and I hate that.

Estela shook her head and looking at her, said seriously:

– I don't understand you!

Lowering her voice, a little, Renata asked:

– Did you stay here the whole time? Did you notice if any arguments happened around here? Everything was fine?

– Everyone is cheerful, and the party is wonderful. Why do you ask?

– It's just that I promised mom I would take care of everything, and I stayed out there for a long time, resting. Come on, let's go for a walk around the hall, to see if everything is alright.

As they circulated around the salon and chatted with some friends, stopping here and there, Renata scanned the place in search of the young woman and the young man who were arguing in the garden. Even though she had redoubled her attention, she was unable to identify either of them. She searched the profiles of the people scattered around the party for some trace that would make her identify the couple whose argument she had witnessed in the garden. She searched the faces of the young women for some trace of anguish, disappointment or anger, and the boys for a hint of annoyance. What she did not know, however, was that human emotions are not always so obvious.

The party ended and, on the way home, Renata continued to think about the matter. She felt that this story could end badly and, that night, in bed, before falling asleep, the young woman sent the unknown couple energies of understanding and peace through her usual prayers.

✳ ✳ ✳

Sunday dawned rainy, and Renata woke up not wanting to get up. The young woman closed her eyes, trying to sleep a little longer, but she failed. She finally decided to get up, take a bath and go downstairs for coffee.

Arriving at the dining room, Renata saw that the table was covered with many small bites and cake, reminding her of the party the day before. The young woman sat down, poured herself coffee with milk and a piece of cake. As she ate, she was suddenly reminded of the couple's dialogue that she overheard unintentionally. Curiosity returned, and she began to go over in her mind some loving couples she knew socially but came to no conclusion.

Margarida approached and said cheerfully:

– From Paulo José's comments, the party must have been wonderful! I kept imagining everything. Your parents are still sleeping. They must have had a lot of fun.

– Yes, it was very nice.

– You don't seem the least bit excited! You who love to dance! Didn't you have fun?

Renata shrugged her shoulders.

– Not much. I like to dance, to feel the music, to enter its harmony, but young men only want to hold me tight, to sigh and say things in my ear, to woo me, and that's not what I expect to find when I agree to dance. If I had a partner who thought like me, who was light, cheerful, natural, I would have had more fun.

– When that wrinkle forms on your forehead, it's a sign that you really didn't like the party.

Renata looked around and verifying that no one was around, lowered her voice:

– I was shocked by a conversation I ended up overhearing unintentionally in the garden.

In a few words, Renata told Margarita what she heard and finished:

– I was afraid that she would do what she had promised and put an end to our party, but, happily, that did not happen. I even tried to find out who the couple was, observing the faces of the people in the room, trying to identify something that would remind me of the upset after an argument, but I didn't succeed.

– You were impressed. You will see that even that happened and they understood each other.

– Yes, I'm going to forget about it, in the end, I have nothing to do with it.

– Paulo José is with some friends at the pool. It's a nice day! Go be with them.

Renata did not respond to Margarita's suggestion, limiting herself to finish eating. After drinking her morning coffee, she went to the library, grabbed a book, settled into a comfortable armchair and began to read.

She didn't like her brother's friends, always so boisterous, discussing what was new at the theaters, the latest movies, which usually ended in mean–spirited and gratuitous criticisms. That was what bothered her. They frequented the best shows in town and, instead of taking advantage of the good moments that art provided, they always sought to highlight the worst of everything. And when they couldn't find anything, they would go beyond that, picking apart the personal lives of some of the artists.

Paulo José never left their side. They were always confabulating, talking quietly, and Renata did not feel at ease in their company. When questioned by her brother, who demanded that she pay more attention to her friends, Renata politely avoided them.

She was busy reading and listened:

– Is this where you are hiding? I was wondering why a pretty girl like you would do that.

Frowning, Renata looked at the boy who was smiling at her and replied:

– And I didn't expect you to invade my privacy uninvited.

Nelson bit his lips, looked at her seriously and turned:

– Sometimes you need to be bold. The day is beautiful, and I don't understand how a healthy young woman like you prefers to stay locked inside the house. I came to invite you to join our group. Maria Alice and Beatriz are also with us.

Renata put the bookmark in the book, closed it and looked seriously at Nelson:

– I always do what I like. For the moment, I prefer to continue reading this book, so if you give me permission, I would like to finish what I was doing.

– I insist, Renata. Every time I come here, I keep expecting to see you around and I always leave frustrated. Just don't want to stay with the group, at least, accept to walk around with me, to walk a little. I love your presence. You are different from all the other girls I live with. I would really like to get to know you better.

Renata placed the book on the side table, stood up and, facing him, replied:

– Your insistence is distasteful to me, Nelson. If I wanted to be with you or your friends, I would have gone. I have already said that I want to continue reading and I do not wish to be discourteous to you. Leave me alone.

Nelson's eyes flashed spitefully, as he said, "You don't want to, but you're being very rude:

– You don't want to, but you are being very impolite. No one has ever done that to me. You're still going to have to answer for what you're doing.

Nelson turned his back on her, walked out and went to meet his friends

Renata felt slightly dizzy, as shivers ran through her body. The young woman sat up and ran her hand over her forehead, wanting to push the bad feeling away.

She got up, took a deep breath, went into the dining room and drank a glass of water. Then, she went to the bedroom and, leaning against the door, sat down on the side of the bed, closed her eyes and tried to detach herself from her inner world in search of balance

Renata knew that within her soul there was a divine essence and that, by binding herself to it, she was binding herself to God. She always did that; all the evil was gone. The young woman felt inspiration, and the answers to her questions came clear in her mind, as if someone was conversing with her. Renata let herself stay a few minutes in that spiritual communication with the light and, little by little, she got better.

Everything passed, and she felt much better, but when she thought of her brother, she felt a tightness in her chest and began to wonder:

– Why does Paulo José like the company of those evil friends with such a bad vibe?

Renata knew that people come together by affinity, which meant that Paulo José was probably just like the friends and vibrated in the same tune as those boys. What she once considered to be just youthful pranks, she now felt could be something more serious, in the end everything is united, connected. All types of energies circulate in space, both high and inspirational as well as deleterious, and Paulo José, apparently, is always linked to those of low vibration.

Renata began to remember situations in which Paulo José was involved, some attitudes, and she only asked God intimately that the brother had the opportunity to raise his vibration, because evil has several sides, and all of them lead to suffering. Only good does good, and evil causes evil. A negative thought is enough to create negative energies that materialize in the body, causing discomfort and other unpleasant situations.

—Where did I learn all that?" she asked herself, and, vaguely, the face of the woman from the dream came to her mind. Renata felt, then, that she was the one who taught her that.

Renata thought of Paulo José again and was taken by the certainty that, as much as she wanted to protect her brother, she did not have that ability, because she knew that people are the only ones responsible for choosing their own path, the way they want to live, and she had no way to avoid that.

The young woman closed her eyes and decided to keep her thoughts elevated, positive. She had already used that technique a few times in small things and succeeded, then, she linked herself to the light of her soul and imagined her brother saying goodbye to his friends, very happy, surrounded by better and true people. She decided that she would do the exercise every day to try to help her brother in some way. She would lose nothing by trying.

After that, Renata went back to the living room, grabbed the book and continued reading.

CHAPTER 2

Renata opened the bedroom door, but no one was there. Despite everything, she clearly heard the knocking and wondered: "Could it be that it was a dream?" Even though it was already dawn, the silence made her believe that everyone was still asleep. It was seven o'clock in the morning and, since it was a Sunday, a day when everyone got up later, especially Paulo José, who always arrived when the day was already light, Renata concluded that it was Margarita who knocked at the door.

The young woman put on her camisole and went to the kitchen. There was no one there either. Intrigued, Renata stood in front of Margarita's room and, noticing that she had already woken up, knocked on the door. Shortly after, the face of the maid appeared through the ajar door:

– It's you. Did something happen?

– That's what I'm asking you. Why did you knock on the door of my room?

– Me?! I didn't knock! I finished getting dressed and I didn't even get dressed yet.

– Someone knocked on my door. I heard it very well. If it wasn't you, who could it have been?

– I didn't hear anything, Renata. You'll see it was a dream.

– Yes, maybe it was.

– I'm going to get dressed and make coffee. It's Maria's day off... Why don't you sleep some more?

– I'm sleep deprived. I'm going to take a bath, then coffee.

Half an hour later, Renata walked to the kitchen, attracted by the tasty smell of coffee. The table was set in the dining room, and she made herself comfortable. She poured the coffee with milk, and as she was spreading butter on the bread, Francisco, the driver, appeared in the kitchen shouting:

– Help, help me!

The two women ran scared, and Margarita asked:

– What happened?

– Paulo José is lying in the garden and seems to be dead!

– Let's go and see him! said Renata, frightened.

Francisco went out, and the two women accompanied him to a corner of the garden. Paulo José was unconscious, with torn clothes and blood on them.

Frightened, Renata placed her hand on his chest:

– Thank God, he's still breathing! Margarita, go call daddy, while I stay with him. Quick!

– Shall we carry him inside?

– No. It's better not to move him and call the doctor.

Shortly after, Dionísio arrived frightened on the scene.

– What's happened?

– I don't know, dad! He's unconscious. I called his name several times, but Paulo didn't answer me.

Renata smelled a strong odor of drink but preferred not to comment on it. Dionísio put his hand on his son's forehead.

– It's freezing! And this blood in the bag?! Maybe it was an assault? I'm going to call Dr. Leocadio and ask for help!

– Let me go, Dad. Stay with him in the meantime. Removing him may worsen his situation.

Renata was talking to the doctor, when Eunice emerged frightened:

– What's going on, why did your dad run out of the room alone wearing his pajamas?

Renata signaled her to wait, ended the call and explained:

– Francisco found Paulo José lying in the garden, passed out, and Dad was with him. I just called Dr. Leocadio and asked him to come here as a matter of extreme urgency.

Eunice turned pale and said nervously:

– Where are they? I want to see him; I need to see my son!

Renata took her there.

– The doctor is on his way.

Seeing her son in that state, Eunice staggered and said nervously:

– He's bad, he looks dead!

Dionísio looked at his daughter and asked her:

– Renata, go get a painkiller for your mom.

Margarida intervened:

– I have a very good painkiller. I will get it.

– It is better to go with her – Dionisio asked Eunice.

– I'm not leaving here until I know what he has.

– All right, I'm going to look for him – Margarita decided.

Margarida moved away, while Francisco, fearing that Eunice would faint, placed a chair in the garden to accommodate her.

While they waited for Dr. Leocadio to arrive, Renata entered the house and sat down near the telephone, wondering if it would not be better to call an ambulance. It was Sunday, and the doctor might be delayed. She was undecided, when she heard someone say.

– It's urgent. Call an ambulance.

Immediately, Renata called the hospital and asked for help. Then she closed her eyes and connected with God, asking for spiritual help. She felt calmer and went back to talk to her father.

– I called Dr. Leocadio. He woke up recently but offered to come.

– Paulo José is still unconscious. I tried to revive him, but he did not react.

– The doctor may be delayed. I called the hospital and asked for an ambulance.

– You did well. This waiting is killing me!

– Calm down, Dad! It may not be serious.

Half an hour later, Dr. Leocadio arrived and began to examine the boy, while the others waited anxiously, their eyes fixed on him.

– So, doctor, how is he?

The doctor shook his head:

– Very weak. He lost a lot of blood. It is better to remove him to a hospital.

Before they answered, the ambulance siren sounded, and the doctor asked:

– Open the gate. They will have to enter to put him on the stretcher.

Dionisio stood up:

– While they provide for his removal, I am going to get dressed to accompany them.

The doctor intervened.

– I will go with the ambulance. You can get dressed and go at once.

The nurses had already placed Paulo José in the ambulance, and the doctor said goodbye:

– I'll meet you there. Let's go.

Dionísio put his hand on the doctor's arm.

– Do whatever it takes, but don't let my son die!

The doctor did not answer, he hugged him quickly and got into the ambulance, which left the house sounding the siren to open the way.

Eunice, her face wet with tears, had to be sheltered until she reached home. Renata and Margarita helped her, while Dionísio hurried to change his clothes. While the daughter and the maid comforted Eunice, he dressed quickly and went downstairs. Seeing him arrive ready to leave, Eunice said in distress:

– I'll go with you, wait for me!

– You are not well. It's better to stay here. So, when I get there, I'll give you news.

– I'll go anyway! I want to be near my son. You must wait for me!

– I can't wait for you. I'm too anxious. He may need me.

Renata intervened:

– Mom wants to be near him, Dad, but I understand your opinion. You can go. We'll change our clothes and go right away.

– It's better this way.

Dionísio left in a hurry, while Renata and Margarita sheltered Eunice, who was trembling and frightened. She was quickly taken to the room.

Margarida wanted to go with them, but Renata asked her to stay and take care of the house and promised that she would inform her as soon as they had news of the sick person.

During the trip to the hospital, Renata, holding her mother's hand, prayed silently. Although she felt that the situation was serious, she was confident that her brother would recover.

Feeling that this aggression could be the result of Paulo José's attitudes made her uncomfortable. Renata knew that everyone always reaps what they sow, and she often felt how the brother had a weak side, preferring the company of light and evil people to those with good feelings. At that moment, she felt how much she loved him and wrapped him with much love, imagining him recovered, cheerful, strong and healthy.

When Renata and Eunice arrived at the hospital, they went straight to the reception, looking for news of Paulo José. The two soon saw Dionísio in the corridor, waiting for the result of the exams. Mother and daughter went to meet him, who, upon seeing them, stood up and embraced his wife.

– So, then, how is she? – Eunice asked anxiously.

–He is receiving a blood transfusion, while they do some tests. He hasn't woken up yet.

– My God, he must be in a bad way!

– Don't say that, Mom. Let's think about what's best. He'll come and he'll be fine. Paulo needs good energy to recover.

Dionísio took a deep breath, trying to calm down:

– This waiting is desperate, but I agree with Renata. We need to hope for the best. Not for a second, I don't want to think about the worst. He will get well, for God is great.

Eunice sighed trying to calm down and did not answer. Time went by, and the doctor did not show up. Two hours later, the door opened, and Dr. Leocadio approached. The three of them got up anxiously, afraid to ask about Paulo José's condition. Despite that, Dionísio took the risk:

– And then, doctor, what do you have?

– He was shot at the level of the pancreas. The bullet hit him and went through. As he took a long time to be treated, he lost a lot of blood. The surgery went well, but we must wait. For now, Paulo is sedated and continues to receive blood transfusions.

– My God, who would have done that? – Eunice asked, distressed.

– Also, we informed the police of what happened, and they will hear our statements later. For the moment, we will only take care of Paulo's recovery. In an hour, if everything goes well, he can be transferred to the room. We need to talk to the secretary and make the admission – clarified the doctor.

Dionísio wanted to go deeper into the matter, but, because he was in front of the family, he held back. He would find out more later.

– He would find out more later. I will take care of all that – he quickly answered the doctor.

– You do that. I need to leave, but my assistant will stay by your side, and we will keep in touch.

– I want to know everything that happened – Dionisio asked.

– Stay calm. I think Paulo will be fine. He is young, strong and healthy and he will react. I am sure of that. Let's wait.

The doctor left, and, after regularizing the situation at the secretary's office, Dionísio proposed:

– While we wait, let's have a coffee, have something to eat.

– I am not hungry. I don't want to eat anything, said Eunice.

– Well, my stomach is empty. A coffee with milk would do me good – reinforced Renata.

– We all need to feed ourselves. We must be well enough to take care of Paulo. He will need us – decided Dionísio.

Eunice sighed:

– You are right. We need to be well, because we don't know what's coming.

– He will get better, mom. We need to think of the best. He's alive, getting treatment. He's healthy, strong, he's going to recover. I'm sure of that.

✴ ✴ ✴

In the cafeteria, while they ate, Eunice continued to be unhappy with what happened to her son and searched for an explanation for that difficult situation.

– Who would have done that? Why would they shoot Paulo? Would it have been a robbery?

— I don't think so. If it was a robber, he would have taken his watch, his wallet, but nothing was taken. The police need to investigate the case and find out what happened. I won't be calm until they find out why they tried to kill Paulo!

Renata felt a tightness in her chest but said nothing. She had been asking herself that same question ever since she saw her brother lying on the floor.

After having a snack in the company of Eunice and Renata, Dionísio went to the surgical center to talk to the doctor. He was informed that his son was well, but that he would continue some more time under observation.

— If everything continues well, in an hour, he will be able to go to his room. Take the opportunity to get some rest.

The room was already available, and everyone headed for it. Renata settled her mother on a sofa and sat down next to her, trying to appear calm to instill courage in her. Dionísio and Eunice's apprehension was evident.

Sitting in a corner of the room, Dionísio's chest felt tight. Inwardly, he wondered what motivated that crime, after all, Paulo José was always very well regarded in society, he had good friends, he was respected, he never did wrong to anyone or got involved in bad things, however, it was evident that that attack was not an assault. Someone had shot him to kill! But who? How would they find out the truth?

Noticing the nervousness of Dionísio and Eunice, Renata, in her thoughts, asked her spiritual friends to strengthen the parents so that they could face the situation with courage.

An hour and a half later, the nurses entered the room bringing Paulo José on a stretcher. Dionísio, Eunice and Renata, stood up at the same time, while the patient was placed on the bed.

– Is he better? – asked Dionísio.

– The doctor will come later to inform you about the patient's condition, sir.

Eunice, approaching from the bed, said nervously:

– He is so pale! Isn't it better to call the doctor soon?

– The patient is still sedated, ma'am, and the pallor is natural due to blood loss. Even with transfusions, it will take some time for his condition to normalize. The doctor released him from the ICU, which is a good sign. Eunice looked at her son's face, then fixed it on the nurse and asked:

– Is the doctor going to be late?

Dionísio intervened:

– Calm down, Eunice. If he were not well, the doctor would have left him longer in the ICU.

The nurse smiled.

– Likewise. Good night, Eunice.

As the nurses took Paulo José to the room, Renata saw Norma next to her brother and felt relieved. She then closed her eyes and said in thought:

– How good to see you, Norma, is Paulo going to recover?

– What happened with Paulo was a warning for him not to run away from his responsibilities. That's all I can tell you.

– I feel that he is in danger and that I haven't done much to help him, Norma. I'd like to help him, Norma. What can I do?

– Wrap him in love, Renata. Get closer to him, try to get on his good side. You're a master at that.

– All right. I'll do what I can! I'll do my best! Thank you.

Half an hour later, the doctor arrived and the three of them got up anxiously. Dionysius wanted to know:

– Is he going to be alright, doctor? What is my son's diagnosis?

– Despite having lost a lot of blood, I think he will recover. He is young, strong.

Distressed, Eunice intervened:

– Will my son be able to lead a normal life?

– Calm down, Mrs. Eunice. The worst is over.

The doctor approached the bed, took Paulo José's pulse in his hands and confirmed the pulsation. Then, he gently opened the young man's eyelids and made notes on the chart hanging from the bed. Finally, he turned to the three, who remained with their eyes fixed on him, and considered:

– He will have no sequelae. The human body is so perfect that he will be able to overcome what happened. What worries me is how he will react emotionally to the event.

When he is better, it would be advisable to seek the help of a psychiatrist.

– Is he going to be slow to wake up? – Eunice asked.

– The anesthesia is wearing off, but he will take a mild painkiller and will only wake up tomorrow, as he needs to rest and get well to talk about what happened. The police commissioner said he will be back tomorrow afternoon to hear his side of the story.

– And is he able to do that?

– I think he is. In any case, I will be around, and I will only allow that meeting if he is well. Now I need to leave.

After the doctor left, Dionísio looked at his watch and said:

– It's late, it's already past ten o'clock. You two must be tired. It's better to go home, I'll stay here.

– I will not move from here in any way. You go home with Renata. Doctor Leocadio said that Paulo will spend the night sleeping, but if there is any news, I'll call and let you know.

– I'm not going to leave you alone, Eunice. You are tired, nervous, dejected. You need to relax, to rest. Go home with Renata, rest and come back early tomorrow. I'm fine and not sleepy, I can stay.

– It's no use. I won't leave here until my son is better.

– In that case, I'll walk Renata home and come back to keep you company.

– Dad, you can stay here with mom. Francisco is out there ready and can take me home – suggested the young woman.

– Do you think you'll be alright?

– Yes. Try to rest. Tomorrow morning, I'll be back. If you need me to buy or bring anything, just let me know.

Renata kissed her brother's forehead, hugged her mother affectionately and Dionísio accompanied her to the car. Francisco was anxious, waiting for news of the young man. The chauffeur, discreet, polite and well behaved, had been working for the family for more than eight years and was loved and respected.

– He's going to be alright! God is great! – he exclaimed in relief.

– Renata needs rest. Take care of her, Francisco. I ask you to take her safely home and, if you notice anything strange, call the police. We don't know exactly what happened, nor the reason for that shot Paulo José took. We don't know who we are dealing with.

– You can rest assured, doctor! I'll stay pending and ask Margarita to take care of Mrs. Renata.

✳ ✳ ✳

At home, Margarida, anxious, was waiting for them. When Renata arrived, the woman embraced her with affection.

– How are things at the hospital? Is Paulo José going to be alright?

– He underwent surgery, had some transfusions because he lost a lot of blood due to the bullet wound and is still sleeping. He is still sedated, but Dr. Leocadio said that he will certainly recover.

– Are you sure he will be alright?

– Yes. As he is stable, he didn't even stay in the ICU. He is already in the room. The doctor gave him a sleeping pill, because he wants him to rest and wake up tomorrow without pain.

– That's good! But you are down.

– I'm tired, Margarida. That's all. The scare was great, but now I'm calmer. I just need to rest.

– Before resting, you need to eat something. I prepared that soup you like so much. Have at least one plate of it.

– I'm not hungry.

– But you will eat, because you need to regain your energy. Or do you want your parents to have to take care of two sick children?

– Ok. I am going upstairs to take a bath and come back for some soup.

– I'll take it to your room myself.

Renata kissed her lightly on the cheek.

– Thank you. It's good to have you here, Margarida!

Later, Margarida stayed in the room talking to Renata, while the young woman had her soup and gave her details of the events. After the woman left with the tray, Renata stretched out on the bed, thought of her brother and felt again a tightness in her chest.

–He's not well! she thought. That bad energy is upon him.

Renata closed her eyes and raised her thoughts, trying to contact her spirit guide. She thought of the brother, and a wave of anger enveloped her. Then by means of an astral projection, she saw herself in the hospital room and over his head a shadow that looked like a man, whose face she could not see. From that shadow, came rays that wrapped Paulo José's body. Renata, then, approached the bed and put her hand on her brother's head and asked the friendly spirits for help.

As he fell asleep, Paulo José seemed not to register that presence, but Renata, observing those energies penetrating the brother's body, kept asking for the help of the spirituality to intercede for the boy. In His perfect laws, God always provides us with the help of good friends of light to appease our afflictions and anguish.

Shortly after, Norma and Jose entered the room, and immediately a wave of light enveloped the shadow that instantly disappeared. The two then extended their hands over Paulo José, and Renata, in spirit, joined them in prayer. The boy's breathing, which was a bit heavy, was getting smoother.

Eunice, despite having stretched out on the sofa, was restless and could not get to sleep. Overcome by fatigue, the woman dozed off for a while, but soon woke up frightened, stirred, feeling her heart racing.

Sitting in an armchair Dionísio, sleepless, watched over his wife and son, but he could not overcome his fear of the future. He had no doubt that someone had shot Paulo Jose to kill him. Everything indicated that it was not an attempted robbery, that the shot had been fired for another reason. And since the shooter failed, he could try again. The risk persisted.

Dionísio wondered what steps he would have to take to prevent this from happening again, and now he was thinking of Renata who was alone in the house, in the company of the servants. He did not know if his daughter was also at risk, so his fear grew. Was that shot made with the intention of killing Paulo José or to hit him? Were Renata and Eunice's lives also at risk? Anguish only increased in the heart of the family patriarch.

The three spirits in prayer enveloped the couple with energies of light and love, and Eunice finally managed to fall asleep. Although Dionísio was unable to sleep, he began to feel a little calmer and set about protecting the family in every way he could. He would hire experienced professionals to work in parallel with the police to find out who had been the aggressor. It was getting light when Dionísio finally managed to relax and fall asleep.

The three then left the hospital. Norma and José accompanied Renata leading her back to the body, and then they rose towards infinity.

CHAPTER 3

The next morning as soon as she woke up Renata called the hospital to find out how her brother had spent the night and Eunice informed her that Paulo José still had not woke up. The boy had been submitted to some tests and after evaluating the results the doctor said that everything was going well and that soon the boy would wake up. After finding out about her brother's condition Renata informed her mother that after the breakfast she would go to the hospital with Margarida.

The girl was just hanging up the phone when her father arrived home. Shaken and worried, Dionísio said, before even being asked by his daughter:

– I just came to take a bath and change my clothes. I'm going back to the hospital in a little while. The delegate will take Paulo José's statement and I want to follow everything.

– Margarida and I will go there too, Dad. We could go together.

– I can't stay long, daughter. If you want to go with me, be ready when I come down.

Fifteen minutes later Dionísio came downstairs. The two women were waiting for him in the pantry and Renata put her arm around her father.

– Dad, we are having breakfast. Yesterday you spent the whole day without eating anything and we all need to be well to take care of Paulo José. Come, Margarida made that pancake you like so much.

– Ok, but we can't stay long.

While they were eating Renata wrapped her father with energies of warmth and peace.

– These pancakes are very good, Margarida! You've outdone yourself today! Congratulations!

Margarida's lips opened in a sweet smile.

– You were hungry! That was it!

– Don't be modest! I even had two pancakes! – Renata smiled back.

– It was good that I fed myself! I'm feeling much better!

Renata smiled, thanking the spirituality for all the guidance she was receiving and that it was helping her to take care of her family.

✳ ✳ ✳

When the three of them entered the hospital room Eunice stood up saying:

– I am glad you are here. I don't like to be alone. All kinds of bad thoughts come to me.

– You're tired, Eunice! You didn't sleep at all last night. You need to go home, take a bath, eat properly and rest. I'm feeling better after I did that. I'll stay here with him so that you can go home and recuperate.

Renata intervened:

– Margarida made those pancakes you like so much. They are wonderful. We brought you some, and you'd better eat them before they get cold.

– I'm not hungry. It feels like I have a cake in my stomach.

Dionísio opened the container with the pancakes and offered them to his wife:

– Eat, it is still warm. You will feel better. We need to be strong to take care of Paulo José.

In order not to disappoint them Eunice started to eat the pancakes prepared by Margarida.

–Hum, they are really good! she thought as she fed herself.

Half an hour later Paulo José started to move around in bed and put his hand on the arm where they had placed the access for the IV and the medications. Renata held her brother's hand and said:

–Calm down, everything is fine. The worst is over

Anxious, Eunice, Dionísio and Margarida approached the bed. Still stunned, the boy opened his eyes and asked:

– What happened? Where am I? What is this place?

Dionísio answered:

– You are in the hospital, son. You underwent surgery but everything is fine.

– Father, I'm dizzy.

– You're still weak and taking too many medications. Stay calm.

Paulo José's voice was pasty and a little croaky. The sick man then closed his eyes and fell asleep again.

The nurse who arrived at that very moment to administer some medicine to him took the boy's pulse. Shortly thereafter he opened one of his eyes slightly. The woman explained:

– He is coming to his sense and will soon be fully awake.

An hour later Paulo José woke up fully complaining about the pain he felt in his stomach. He abruptly raised his head and became dizzy.

Renata lifted the headboard, adjusted the pillows to accommodate him better and said:

– You can't get up yet, my brother.

– I'm feeling a lot of pain.

Eunice called the nurse who brought a pill and made the boy take it. She explained:

– It will still hurt a little but be patient. Soon you will be better.

As soon as the nurse left, Dionisio sat down on the side of the bed, stared at his son and asked:

– Do you remember what happened?

Paulo José thought for a while and then as if trying to do a quick retrospective of the last events he remembered, said more to himself:

– I left the party at Julinhos's house early in the morning, I don't remember the time very well. I arrived home, opened the gate, drove into the garage and as I was walking towards the door a figure came out from behind the wall. I saw that he had a gun and I felt that he was going to shoot me. I wanted to run away but I couldn't. I heard two loud bangs and felt a strong burning sensation in my stomach and something hot soaking my clothes. I felt dizzy and fell. I wanted to scream, to call someone, it was horrible. Then I don't remember anything else. Just waking up here. Do you know what happened, who did that?

Dionísio shook his head negatively.

– Not yet. I don't know how long you were lying there, son. It was Francisco who found you unconscious and came to call us. Doctor Leocadio helped you and brought you here. Then, you underwent surgery and some blood transfusions that saved your life.

A wave of emotion passed over Paulo José's face and he remained silent for a few seconds. He asked:

– Was the surgery to extract the bullets?

– No son. The bullets went through your body. They extracted some fragments but the shells themselves were found on the ground. Son, everything went well. The important thing is that you won't have any after–effects.

Paulo José remained silent for a few more seconds and then commented:

– I never imagined that this could happen to me!

– The police are already investigating the case. The delegate will come here today to question you and try to get some leads.

– It had to be a robbery, Dad. Those bandits are losing all around us.

– The police believe that it was not a robbery, after all, whoever shot you took absolutely nothing. The money was in your wallet, the watch was still on your wrist when we found you, and that gold pen that you like to carry in your inside jacket pocket was there too. Do you know anyone who is envious or angry with you? Try to remember, son, that person shot to kill you! I have also been going through my mind trying to find someone who might have done that to get to me. I am worried.

Paulo José was thoughtful for a few seconds and then shook his head negatively, saying:

– I have no enemies, Dad! It can only have been a robbery.

– The police believe there is another motive. This person didn't enter the house or try to take anything. Not even the car was taken.

– Maybe someone in the house woke up, opened a window, and he got scared and ran away.

When Renata heard what the brother was saying, she felt a tightness in her chest and asked herself why her brother was trying to make her father and the family believe this hypothesis. Paulo José did not want to open about what he knew did not want to voice his doubts. It seemed as if he was trying to stop the investigation. Renata then thought that the danger of a new assassination attempt continued and that the motive of that attempt was not clear.

While Dionísio was talking to Paulo José, explaining to him what the doctor had said about the surgery, Renata remembered the discussion she had heard in the garden the night of the party. She could not see the couple because she was on a bench behind a flowering hedge. She had only heard the argument and the altered voices but did not know who the owners of those voices were.

Renata wondered if this had anything to do with the attack against her brother. –" Is Paulo Jose' somehow involved in that case?" she asked herself. Paulo José was the leader of the group of friends and always defended them in any situation. She did not like the guys who lived around him, fawning him and taking advantage of his good life.

If the boy that the girl threatened was one of Paulo José's friends, he would certainly get involved on his behalf. Could this have been the cause of the attack?

The more she thought about the subject the more Renata became convinced that her brother was involved in the case. However, she did not believe that the brother was the father of the girl's child. He circulated with many women, promise them nothing, and only enjoyed the games they played to win him over. He had never dated anyone, however. Renata believed that her brother would not be so inconsequential as to get a girl pregnant.

Still absorbed in her thoughts Renata decided that when Paulo José was better and no one was around, she would have a talk about what had happened the night of the party and then she would know if her suspicions had any basis.

※※※

On the afternoon of that day, the delegate finally showed up accompanied by a clerk to take Paulo José's statement. The convalescent boy wanted to sit down but the nurse raised the head of the bed a little and gave him directions:

– It is best not to force the wound site. Remember that you had both internal and external stitches. I will help you. Lie back carefully and do not strain yourself.

Paulo José lifted his head slowly, felt a little dizzy, and the nurse put another pillow behind the boy's head to keep him supported. She asked:

– How do you feel?

– A little weak.

Observing the policemen who were seated next to the bed where the boy was lying, she considered:

– It would be better to leave this interrogation until tomorrow.

The delegate shook his head:

– Impossible! The shots were meant to kill! Since he didn't succeed, the killer could come back. We must clarify some facts. Paulo, did you have an argument, a fight with someone?

– No. I'm of peace, delegate. I believe I was victimized by someone who entered the property to steal but was surprised by me. I was returning from a party at my friend Julinho's house. I arrived at our house at dawn.

– Did you see the element who fired the shot?

– No. I had drunk a little bit, after all I was at a party, and I didn't see anything. I just heard the shots; felt a strong burning in my stomach and lost consciousness. Then I woke up here. That's all I can tell you.

The delegate was thoughtful for a few seconds and then said:

– Look boy, in this world there are many envious people.... you are a boy of high society, and you may have aroused the greed of others. There are many unbalanced and loose people out there who, when they don't have access to something, end up trying to destroy the other. Besides all of this, your dad is an important criminal lawyer and may have messed with dangerous people, which would justify the attack you suffered. These are still guesses. That shot may have come from people close to you or from someone who wanted to harm your dad. We are used to dealing with cases like this and arresting the culprits. Once we have ruled out an attempted robbery, we must think of other possibilities, so don't be afraid to tell us the truth. We know how to deal with these cases.

Paulo José did not answer immediately, and the delegate waited in silence. Then the boy said

– I don't believe these hypotheses. To me, it was just an attempted robbery.

– That almost cost you your life. You are alive and that will certainly displease your executioner. Don't you think you are taking a risk?

– I intend to ask my father to hire an armed security guard to protect our family. If that thief shows up, he will be arrested!

The delegate was silent for a few seconds, then said:

– When you fell wounded, he was armed and could have surrendered everyone in the house and stolen whatever he wanted. Why didn't he do it then? He didn't even take your wallet and your personal belongings.

– I think someone in the house may have heard a noise and opened a window. That's all it could have been.

The delegate looked at him seriously, then, turning to the clerk, asked:

– Did you take note of our conversation?

– Yes, doctor.

– Give it to him to sign.

The clerk carefully placed the paper on a book and asked Paulo José to check the statement. Then he explained:

– I will go through your statements and come back for you to sign.

Renata had heard to the entire conversation and clearly noticed that Humberto, the delegate, would not be convinced of anything Paulo José said. When they left the room, Renata accompanied them and, in the hallway said seriously:

– Did you accept my brother's hypothesis?

– Why do you ask?

– Because I did not believe what he said either.

– Do you know anything else, and would you like to tell me about it?

– No, but I would like to talk a little more to you and help my brother.

– We could go to the cafeteria where we could talk better.

Renata accompanied him to the cafeteria. They found a table further away, sat down and she began to talk:

– Paulo José has many friends and is not very selective. Just as he has balanced friends in his relationships, he also has sycophants and jockers. My brother feeds his vanity a bit with these friends, but he is not a bad boy. Recently, I have noticed that he does everything to protect these friends even when they do something wrong. I feel that's not right. I've tried to get his attention, but he doesn't take it seriously.

Renata fell silent thoughtfully and the delegate asked:

– Explain better...

– I did not believe the version he has been holding. It was clear that the motive was not robbery.

– Why do you think he gave this version?

– To protect someone.

– Do you suspect who it is?

– I have no proof of anything, but I know how my brother usually acts. Did you believe what he said?

– For now, I'm just checking the facts. Keep watching your friends and be aware of what each one thinks about the case. When they come to visit him at your home, I ask you to pay close attention to their reaction to Paulo José's condition. This could be the way to find the culprit.

– Will you continue to lead with the case?

– It is my job, and your help would be of great use to me. I ask that you contact me directly at this phone. It is not the police station's; it is a private number. Do not pass it on to anyone. I trust your discretion. In investigations, walls have ears!

– Ok.

The delegate said goodbye and Renata thoughtfully returned to her brother's room. The girl still had not mentioned to the delegate the conversation she had overheard the night of the party and was reticent about whether to talk about it or not, although she suspected that the episode might have something to do with the case. She did not believe that her brother was guilty of that story and tried to preserve it. She had talked to Humberto, suggested some possibilities and now she thought it was up to the police to investigate and find the culprit. She felt tranquil because she had done her part.

As a security measure, the delegate had forbidden visits while Paulo José was in the hospital. He was getting better every day and was anxious to receive visits from friends, but he did not get permission. Humberto had explained to Renata that, since Dionísio would signal the possibility of hiring private security guards, the boy would be less vulnerable at home.

***

The hours were passing, and Paulo José was getting more and more irritated for having to stay in the hospital with no one to talk to. Seeing him better and knowing that her son was safe, Eunice started sleeping at home and went to the hospital every morning to give Renata a nap. Dionísio stopped by early in the morning to see his son and then went to work.

Renata returned to the hospital in the afternoon and kept her brother company. She listened to his complaints, tried to distract him and brought him magazines and books to entertain him. Paulo José did not like to read, so the boy would just flip through the magazines and make some comments about the people he knew. Renata noticed that he was anxious to go back home, see his friends and resume his life.

The girl tried to talk to her brother, telling him happy things and attracting his attention to new subjects, but she noticed that he was impatient and irritated because he could not leave the hospital. Noticing her brother's constant restlessness, she intimately connected with her inner world and surrounded Paulo José with energies of peace and light, imagining that time would pass quickly and that he would soon be home.

Renata felt that those moments of solitude had happened so that Paulo José could reflect on the danger he had run and change his attitudes and occupy himself with things that would bring him more joy and balance. The girl felt that happiness is only possible when a person assumes responsibility for his own life, tries to be true in his attitudes and, above all, has faith in God, in life and in himself.

Joy nourishes the spirit and is the source that opens the paths to the best and the doors of progress, allowing the involvement of light and spirituality. Even knowing that Paulo José was still far from these concepts, Renata showered her brother with thoughts of love, imagining that one day he would learn to value the good things in life and would do well.

Renata knew that this is the destiny of all of us and that no one is left behind. That although each one must pay the price for their achievement, progress, however long it takes, always continues and no one is lost. Everyone attains wisdom. This feeling comforted her as it comforted many people in this world, making faith in life, in the good and in the future a beacon that illuminated her path and taught her to move forward and discover what was rightfully hers, according to God's plan.

At that moment a bright pink light came out from Renata's chest and enveloped Paulo José, who closed his eyes and fell asleep while some benevolent figures enveloped him with colored lights and vibrations of love.

CHAPTER 4

A week later, Paulo José was discharged and went home satisfied. Although weak, the fact that he could receive friends, to return to his world with a halo of victim, knowing that he would be received as a hero, gave him a pleasant feeling of victory, after all, he liked to be the center of attention.

That afternoon, several of Paulo José' friends showed up to visit him and after the hugs each one of the boys told their stories about how the case had been talked about in the club and in the groups, they used to go to. Besides the fact that several news articles were published in the newspapers about the case, important magazines did reports about the fact and several hypotheses were raised explaining that the police were still investigating the attack and keeping what was found secret.

In the afternoon when Renata entered Paulo José's room, the boy was already surrounded by some friends. With some exaggerations, the young boy recounted all the sufferings he had been through.

Renata stared at them and said:

– Good afternoon! Paulo José is still recovering so I would like to make a request: comment only on the good things so that he gets well and can continue to improve. It is time to take medicine!

Dionísio had hired a nurse technician to administer the medications and dress Paulo José's. The woman opened the door and said:

– There are a lot of people in this room, and the patient needs calm and rest as he is still convalescing. Mr. Paulo Jose' went through a very delicate time so it is best that he receives few friends at a time and that the conversation is light. No comment on what happened. Please, leave for a while.

Paulo José's friends obeyed the woman's request, who commented with Renata:

– Earlier today he was feverish. I think it was the euphoria of the visits. Mr. Paulo is recovering well. Tomorrow, I won't be able to come because I have to accompany my mother for an examination. I already talked to Dr. Dionísio about it, and he understood the situation. Could you administer the medication in my absence? It is all here in the prescription. Before I leave, I will do the dressing. Don't worry about it. You will only have to give the medication at the times noted.

– Of course! Don't worry about it.

Renata looked at the prescription carefully and read some notes that the nurse's technician had made. The woman continued:

– It is simple. Right now, besides the medication, Mr. Paulo just needs a calm environment, good food and lots of rest. The more he sleeps, the faster he will recover. It is essential for the organism to recover.

– You got it. I will take care of him.

After the nurse left Paulo's friends entered the room again and Renata commented:

– You heard what she said, didn't you?

Paulo José intervened:

– Pay no attention. It is the opposite. I'm tired of being alone with no one to talk to. You can come whenever you want. Maybe tomorrow I can get up and sit in the garden for a while. For me your presence is the best medicine!

Renata did not say anything, but she intimately firmed up her intention to keep an eye and prevent any excesses that her brother might commit.

Sitting in a corner of the room Renata was thinking about how to protect her brother from another attempt. Although Humberto had not commented to her about his suspicions, the girl noticed that the delegate was not convinced that Paulo José had been the victim of a robbery attempted either.

Renata knew that Humberto had his suspicions and theories and wondered if she should tell him about the conversation, she had overheard the night of the party. The more she thought about it, the girl became convinced that Paulo José was still in danger and that the person who tried to kill him could come back to finish what he had started. It was quiet a coincidence that she had heard what the girl said and that her brother had been wounded afterwards. It was not only Renata who feared that.

That same afternoon, Dionísio went to the Federal Police headquarters to talk to one of the directors, Dr. Ignácio de Rezende, head of the secret service, who had been his college classmate. Unhappy with the attempt on his son's life, Dionísio knew that as an important criminal lawyer and having confronted and sent some dangerous criminals to prison, he made many enemies and had been sworn to death by some of them. Because of his career, he suspected that the attack Paulo José had suffered was the result of a vendetta.

After a few minutes of waiting, Dionísio was finally received by Ignácio, who was happy and surprised by the visit of his old college friend.

– Dionísio, my dear! What an honor to meet you again! What brings you here?

– Ignácio, I would like to visit you for more pleasant matters, but today I come here as an old friend who needs your help. As you may have read in the newspapers, my son Paulo José, was attacked in front of our house. He was shot twice and almost died.

– Yes, I heard. I didn't call you because I was involved in a big case and faced chaotic days here at headquarters. And how is your son? Is he still hospitalized?

– No, he's home now. He is fine, recovering. Although the bullets went through his body, they did not hit any vital organs. He just lost a lot of blood.

– And how can I help you, my friend?

– I am worried, Ignácio. Paulo José got away this time, but I'm afraid the bandit will try again. Don't you think so?

– But why do you think this person would try again? What's your hypothesis?

– Paulo José believes he was the victim of an attempted robbery, Ignácio but I'm not convinced of this hypothesis. No money, watch, nothing was taken. When we found him unconscious in the garden everything was with him.

– Yes, it doesn't make sense that it was an attempted robbery since nothing was taken from him. But I ask you again... what is your hypothesis?

– My son lives surrounded by friends; he is a happy, good–nature boy. I don't think he has enemies. What worries me is that due to my profession I deal with dangerous elements and the last case I worked on was very difficult. I even received some death threats during the process. This never scared me, however, after all I have already acted in several cases and this protocol of threats has been part of my routine. I know how to protect myself, but I did not imagine that my son could be affected.

– Do you think that what happened is connected to you?

– It could only have been a revenge against me, Ignácio. Someone may be trying to get at me through my family. Paulo José takes life very well and he doesn't get involved in trouble.

– A death threat should not be ignored, Dionísio. These people are dangerous. Don't underestimate them. Why didn't you go to the police?

– This is not the first time I have received death threats because of my work. A criminal's place is in jail, and I have dedicated all these years to make this happen, but I have also thought that the crime may have had another motivation.

– Besides the hypothesis of revenge, do you have any other suspicions?

– Yes, I do. A few days ago, a woman called my house wanting to talk to Paulo José, but he did not want to talk to her. She insisted, and Margarida talked to the woman. She did not give her name, but she made some threats against Paulo José and hung up the phone. When Eunice commented the case to me, I did not take it seriously. My son is a flirt, he goes around with many women, but he has never assumed anything with any of them. I thought it was just some girl who was hurt by him because he didn't look for her anymore. I don't know...

– You did wrong Dionísio. A woman in love is capable anything!

– My son is not in love with anyone. What he wants is to enjoy life and live it well. He doesn't even have a girlfriend. I mentioned this because I believe that at this moment everything must be considered. I still think however that the attack is related to my work. The case that I won two weeks ago was serious. I managed to raise important evidence against the scoundrel who was eventually convicted. He is in jail and will not be able to get out of jail.

– Do you believe that the attack was motivated by this conviction?

– I am sure of it.

– Could you provide me with the details of this case? I would like to study this case as soon as possible.

– Ok. The process is voluminous. I will make a complete summary and sent it to you as soon as possible.

– You know that I do not work in this field, my friend, but I will do my best to help you. Being emotionally removed from the situation I may be able to see some nuances that you, as the victim's father, are not seeing.

– Thank you very much. This is precisely why I have come tom you for help.

– Rest assured. We will find who did this to your son.

After Dionísio left Ignácio called one of his assistants. Marcos entered the room, sat down in front of the table and waited.

Brunette, tall, broad-shouldered, slightly wavy brown hair that he could not keep in place Marcos was 28 years old and worked for Ignácio on special cases.

In a few words Ignácio summarized the conversation he had with Dionísio and concluded:

– Are you interested in helping me with this case?

– Always Dr. Ignácio! You know I like to keep my head on straight!

Ignácio told Marcos what he knew about Paulo José's case and the conversation he had with Dionísio.

– He is sure of what he said. What do you think?

– I feel that we need to investigate this boy's life further and see if he is really as his father thinks. If we want to avoid another attempt, we have to act fast.

Marcos had graduated in journalism and was interested in justice. As he could not find a job in this area, he took a public contest to work in the Federal Police in an administrative position. As he lived with the boy, Ignácio realized that Marcos was gifted with a profound intelligence and perspicacity and ended up creating the habit of discussing some complex cases with him, and so the boy spent his free time as a kind of support for Ignácio. He did this for pleasure and to keep the investigative nose as a journalist alive. Besides, he was a Spiritualist like him.

– You are right. Would you really like to help us with this case?

Marcos closed his eyes, was silent for a few seconds and then said:

– Yes, Dr. Ignácio! As I told you a few times, having the opportunity to participate behind the scenes of cases like this keeps my mind working. Although I am not working in my field now, I have not stopped being a journalist. I like to go after good stories and above all, to uncover them.

– That's why I'm once again making this invitation to you.

– It is a pleasure for me to help you. Well! Let's get to the case! I need to know all the details, including the names and addresses of everyone involved. Today I will start the analysis of the case and I will give you an answer. My character will start working!

Ignácio laughed and commented:

– What will he do this time?

– Get to know those involved in the case. That's the first step. We're in a hurry, so I will start right now. Give me the name and address of the people in that family and all those involved in the case.

Ignácio told Marcos the entire conversation he had with Dionísio and handed him all the notes he had taken.

– I still do not have much information about the case. At this moment I only have the data that Dionísio gave me. I have here in the office some newspapers from the last few weeks. Look at the news that was published about the attack. As Dionísio is an important and well-known lawyer, the whole story was widely reported.

At the end of the workday, Marcos left carrying a small pile of newspapers and some names written down. The boy then went to his apartment and started the investigation.

When analyzing the news that was published about the case in the newspapers and the notes that Ignácio had taken during the conversation with Dionísio, the way in which Paulo José dealt with friendships caught Marcos' attention. Apparently, he was a very popular guy among his friends, who always did his every wish.

None of these boys worked, but they all enjoyed a high standard of living and were always fashionable. According to Dionísio's account to Ignácio, Paulo José's closest friends were five: Julio was 25 years old; Oscar was 21, whose families were from high society; Horacio was 20, Juan was 21 and Nelson was 24.

The first two were very rich, but the others had no the financial resources to maintain the high standard of living they led. Most likely, Paulo José was supporting them, and maybe therefore they were always around him, doing his bidding.

Looking at the material in front of him, Marcos tried to go deeper into the analysis of these people. Besides the experience he had for having helped Ignácio in several difficult cases, he was a spiritualist, Medium and connected to friendly spirits that inspired and protected him. Spirits of light that spoke about the progress of the world, announcing that a new consciousness had already begun to be implanted on Earth, bringing more knowledge in all areas of society for those who were ready and interested in learning new things. And precisely for that reason, Marcos always offered to help Ignácio. He wanted to learn and put his intelligence at the service of justice, something in which he deeply believed, and above all to understand how people's destinies are connected, how stories intersect, and why some succumb to violence or are victims to it.

As a Medium and spiritualist, Marcos had learned that life has functional laws that maintain the balance of forces in the universe, discipline the evolution of everything and everyone, and that everything always evolves for the best. That each individual is a special being, unique and has his or her own path and that, although there are similarities between people, no two people are alike. Each spirit is free to choose how they want to live but reaps the result of their choices. Whoever has a good head can live better, obtain everything he desires in this new incarnation, and in this way, he learns how life works. While illusions bring suffering, the truth liberates and teaches. That is the trajectory of each spirit in the conquest of its own development.

Since his adolescence, Marcos has had relationships with spirits who protected him and taught him what he needed to know about his sensibility in order to keep his balance even though he was in the world under the influence of the negative energies of less evolved spirits.

The high spirits taught him how things are and affirmed that despite the difficulties and apparent injustices of the world, life always makes everything right. Mark was very touched when they showed him that the bodies that the spirit wore to manifest itself both in the astral world and to reincarnate on Earth were created using high technology by the higher masters, so that wherever he was, he could develop his potential to evolve and defend himself from negative energies.

As the spirit evolves, it develops knowledge while its body develops as needed, helping the spirit to understand how life works so that it can successfully carry out its projects in the world.

Delighted with what he had learned, Marcos studied the laws of life and practiced each one of them, and discovered that even though they have different functions, they complement each other in such a way that the added results bring knowledge, balance, well–being and a comfortable sense of security to people.

After reading once more the newspaper clippings and Ignácio's notes Marcos sat down and began to think about the character he would assume for that investigation.

The next day as soon as Ignácio arrived at work, Marcos knocked on his door. Seeing the boy come in, the man got up to hug him and said happily:

– Well! Excited about the case?

– Yes, very much so!

– Great! I'm happy to have your help again. Let's see if we can help Dionísio to advance in the case. As you may have read in my notes, Paulo José's statement did not convince me, just as it did not convince his father. It was clear that he was not telling the truth. Maybe he is covering up for a friend.

Marcos thought for a while and then said:

– I felt the same way. I am creating a character, Dr. Ignácio. He will be a cheerful lawyer and author of legal books published abroad.

– How will you accomplish that? It won't be easy!

Marcos smiled and his eyes had a mischievous gleam in them when he answered:

– I have everything planned.

– When do you intend to start?

– Soon.

– I think your plan would work better if you don't present yourself as a "famous" person but as an ordinary person. What do you think?

– Well, I think exactly the opposite. I want to arouse curiosity and even a certain fear in them. I want to disturb them. I believe they are covering up the truth about the attack and that Paulo José lied for the delegate. I feel that there is something very serious behind all this and I will find out what this is. That may be the key.

– Anything is possible... Dionísio is an intelligent and astute man. I don't understand why he allows his son to maintain friendships with boys of another level and who are apparently not trustworthy.

Marcos thought for a while and then answered:

– I am sure that he knows what he is doing. I know Dr. Dionísio's trajectory as a criminal lawyer and I know that he is a serious, intelligent and lucid man. I think he trusts his son a lot but understands that he cannot interfere in his son's life that much. Maybe that's why he doesn't oppose Paulo José's friendships.

– You are right.

Marcos stood up and extended his hand to Ignácio.

– I need to go, Dr. Ignácio, because my work is waiting for me here. In the moments I am idle during my workday I will make some more notes and work on my character. I will keep you informed.

– Do that. If you need anything, let me know.

After a handshake Marcos said goodbye and returned to his desk. During lunchtime, he imagined what his new character would be like, and his eyes sparkled with joy. He really liked what he was doing. Being able to prevent evil from manifesting itself was a way of making the world a better place.

At night, when Marcos was already in his apartment, Marcos opened his closet and separated some clothes. He was happy to use his creativity for something good.

✶ ✶ ✶

Since he lived alone and was a federal civil servant, Marcos had a comfortable life. Besides this, a dear aunt who had treated him as her son had left him an inheritance of considerable value that he kept in a savings account. Despite his 28 years of age, Marcos had not married, because he had not found a girl to capture his heart. He then dedicated to work, to help Ignácio with his complex cases, and to study spirituality.

Single and enjoying a financial life without great upsets, Marcos would occasionally indulge in a few luxuries, such as going out to dinner in good restaurants. On these occasions he always dressed elegantly and well, and that night was no different. As it was Friday, he decided he would go out to dinner and looked for an Italian cantina in the Jardins neighborhood. It was after eight o'clock, and the place was packed. The waiter hurried to serve him with pleasure. It was a place where he used to go, and the owner always made a point to greet him.

Marcos sat down at a table and shortly afterwards he had a surprise: two girls entered the restaurant and sat down at a table next to it where it was possible to see a reservation card. On it was written Renata Albuquerque. When he read that name and looked at the girl, he immediately remembered one of the newspaper clippings he had in his hands about the attempt that Paulo José had suffered. In one of them, there was a photo of the girl next with her brother, father and mother.

Marcos stared at her, impressed by the beauty of the girl. Suddenly their eyes met, and he thought: "Yes... the picture in the newspaper does not do justice to the beauty of this girl."

During dinner, Renata felt Marcos's eyes were fixed on her. Even without looking at the boy, she felt his presence.

When they finished dinner and got up to leave, again Renata and Marcos' eyes met, and without wanting to, the girl smiled shyly leaving the restaurant. He wondered, "Why exactly now when I am working on the case involving this girl's family do we meet? What does this mean?" Marcos felt that it could be a message from life signaling that he should start there: by Renata Albuquerque.

CHAPTER 5

A week after that curious encounter with Renata Albuquerque, Marcos went to a fancy club in Rio de Janeiro for a dinner dance. The room was packed when he entered, and the manager accompanied him to a table. As a good observer, the young man ran his eyes over the place, taking in all the details and studying the club's frequenters.

Marcos fixed his attention on the next table, where two girls were chatting. His eyes met Renata's and Isabel, the girl's friend, asked:

– Do you know this boy? His face has changed since he looked at you.

– I thought he looked like a friend of my brother's, but I was wrong.

A young man approached and asked Isabel to dance. Renata got up and went to the toilet, passed by Marcos and, and again, their eyes met. He smelled the delicate perfume emanating from her and kept looking at her until she disappeared among the tables.

Renata sat down, and then Marcos approached the girl and commented:

– I would give a prize to whoever says what is on your mind!

Renata smiled and answered:

– I was trying to find out where we met.

– Maybe it is from other lives.

Renata's eyes sparkled when she answered:

– You look familiar. If we never met in this life, it can only have been in a previous one.

Marcos smiled happily and invited her:

– Shall we dance?

Renata stood up, and Marcos took her hand, wrapped her around her waist and led her to the dance floor. They began to dance, while the orchestra played the blues. Both had the feeling that their feet were not touching the ground. Marcos forgot that he was doing a job and she wanted the music to never end.

With her face flushed and her eyes shining Marcos could not resist and snuggled her even tighter between his arms and Renata, although shy and always so averse to bolder advances from boys, let herself stay. Something sublimes involved them in that encounter – or was it a reunion? When the music stopped, he led Renata to the table where she was sitting.

The girl sat down on a chair and the boy pulled another chair close to him and asked:

– Are you waiting for someone?

– No. I came to accompany Isabel, but I like to go to the club to listen to music.

– You dance very well.

Renata looked at him, smiled slightly and replied:

– In the club it's difficult to find a partner who likes to dance like me. To be in tune with the music is to feel the emotions that it awakens in the soul harmonizes the spirit. It is something that gives me great pleasure. Unfortunately, the partners that come around here, instead of enjoying the moment, prefer to chat and woo me during the dance and the enchantment goes away.

The music started again, and Marcos asked:

– Let's dance then! I would like to experience, to feel the pleasure that music can give us.

Renata got up and, from that moment on, they never stopped dancing. Marcos liked to feel the effect that music had on him and, after a while the two of them were already exchanging ideas about their feelings.

Time passed quickly and Marcos promised to take her home. Renata then asked the driver to take Isabel to her house and excused him from picking her up. It was already dawn when they left the club.

When Marcos parked the car in front of the house, she signaled to the security guard authorizing him to open the gate. After they entered the property Renata stared Marcos, holding out his hand and said:

– This was a special night. Thank you for the company, Marcos.

– You taught me to feel the energies of music. What other good things will we still discover together?

Renata's eyes sparkled; her lips quirked up in a smile as she said:

– This night was different! There's a magic in the air. Didn't you feel it?

Marcos didn't resist, he hugged and kissed her for a long time until she reacted, pulled away and said seriously:

– It's late! I need to get in.

Marcos held Renata's hand, brought it gently to his lips and the boy's voice was soft when he said:

– Sleep with the angels.

While the girl went up the stairs, thinking about the magic of that night, Marcos, who had programmed himself to work on the case of Paulo José's attempt on his life, forgot all about it, fascinated by Renata's beauty and brilliance. He waited for the girl to enter the house, turned around the garden and left with his thoughts immersed in that unforgettable night.

✳︎✳︎✳︎

The next afternoon when the phone rang, Renata felt that it was Marcos. Her heart leapt and she waited a few seconds to answer the call. Trying to control her excitement, she finally took the phone off the hook.

– How are you, Renata?

– I'm very well, and you?

– I thought about you all the time. I feel that we have a lot of things in common and that we need to get to know each other better. Would you like to have dinner with me tonight?

– Of course, I will. What time will you pick me up?

– For me, I'd like to go now.

– You can come after seven. I'll be waiting for you.

– I miss you! I still feel your presence and the emotions of last night.

Renata was thoughtful for a few seconds and then said excitedly:

– I feel that life brought us back together again for a reason and it must have its reasons.

Marcos felt a shiver run through his body and said with emotion:

– Life always knows what it's doing!

✵ ✵ ✵

Just before seven o'clock, Marcos arrived at Renata's house. The security guard opened the gate to the property, and he entered. Dionísio, who was in the living room, looked out the window and, seeing the young man's car parked, opened the door e invited him in.

After the greetings, Dionísio commented:

– So, the young man my daughter met at the club, is you?! I don't quite understand what is going on here. Does all this have to do with the investigation? Ignácio didn't tell me anything about you approaching Renata to get information.

– No, Doctor Dionísio. It has nothing to do with the investigations. I met Renata at the club, we danced and became friends, but she doesn't know I'm working on the case. I would even like to ask your permission to continue seeing her, if that is Renata's wish.

– Well, my boy. I don't know how these stories intersected, but since I trust Ignácio's judgment of you, I will allow you to continue seeing her, if she so desires. I love my daughter and I just want to see her happy. She told me very highly about a boy she met at the club, but I didn't know it was you! Anyway, though, try not to mix things up. I don't want her to get involved in the case because it could be dangerous. I feel that those behind the attack are criminals of the worst kind. I strongly believe in the hypothesis that they wish to take revenge on me, and it is better to leave her out of it.

– Do not worry, Dr. Dionísio. My intentions towards your daughter are the best possible and our affairs have nothing to do with the work I am doing. Don't worry.

– Be sensible! And do you have any news about the attack?

– Not yet. I'm investigating Paulo José's friends to get to know about each one's life.

Without noticing that Dionísio and Marcos already knew each other, Renata went downstairs smiling when she saw her father and the suitor talking in the living room. Marcos stood up to greet her and the girl reciprocated the gesture. Then the girl kissed her father on the cheek and said goodbye.

After saying goodbye to Dionísio, the two left. The patriarch noticed that Marcos' eyes sparkled when Renata appeared beautiful inside a dark green dress that highlighted the light tone of her skin. Thoughtful, Dionísio stared out the window until the car disappeared around the bend in the street. Although the boy and Renata did not belong to the same social class, the patriarch felt that he was a good guy and only wished that if the flirtation went ahead, Marcos would make her happy.

✶ ✶ ✶

– Where are we going? – Renata asked, smiling.

– You choose. What would you like to do?

Renata thought a bit and then said:

– Somewhere quiet, where we can talk.

– I know a very nice restaurant, full of flowers and artwork, where they serve special dishes. There are also musicians who know how to choose songs that touch the soul!

– I would like to know this place – the girl decided.

As soon as they entered the restaurant a very elegant lady welcomed them and led them to the table. The room was very well decorated, with natural flowers and tasteful objects. Very elegant waiters served the tables, and although it was still early, many of them were already reserved. Renata liked what she saw.

The two of them settled down and the conversation flowed pleasantly. Renata loved it when Marcos, in a delicate gesture, kissed her hand and even more when their lips joined. An incredible pleasure enveloped her, and she wished this kiss would never end.

From that night on, that restaurant had become special for the couple. Whenever Marcos asked Renata out, they went to the romantic and dreamy Sunshine.

A few days passed, and Marcos was still focused on the case that Ignácio would present to him. Now that he was involved with Renata, Paulo José's sister, he felt an even greater need to solve the mystery surrounding the attempt on the boy's life. Marcos was researching the routine and lifestyles of all Paulo José's friends who, although still under medical care, had recovered well.

However, something began to bother Marcos: the fact that he was working on the attempt case and did not tell Renata. Each day the boy felt more in love with her and was even thinking of asking her to marry him. At 28 years of age, Marcos wondered why to drag on dating for months or years on end, when he intimately felt that Renata was the great love of his life. But how could he talk about their future without telling her the truth?

Renata was a very truthful woman and the two of them could not get married without him telling her the truth. He thought about it for a while and thought it best to devote himself to the case and try to solve it as quickly as possible so that he could ask her to marry him.

Marcos had made a dossier on Paulo José and his friends in which he wrote down everything he knew about each of them. To begin with he imagined his character as a wealthy, influential lawyer who was spending his vacation in the city.

All day long Marcos worked on his plan to get himself into Paul José's group of friends. To get more information he would need to become one of them. But how to do this without them and Renata finding out? He would have to count on luck and hope that no one would comment on him with the girl.

The boy composed a jocular character, very much to the taste of Paulo José's group. Besides doing a good deed by helping Ignácio, Marcos had fun living these characters. As he was in a hurry, he went out to buy some things he needed.

Eager, the boy decided to start acting that very night. He called Renata and told her that he would need to be away for two or three days due to work.

Then he arranged everything he deeded for his purpose and as was his habit, he settled down on the sofa, closed his eyes, concentrated and listened: `` I know about the case. I am here to help you."

I created a character and wait for your suggestions.

Prepare yourself a little more. Those boys are dangerous Marcos. I suggest you follow up a little more before you start acting directly. They are all dishonest, mean and capable of doing anything to get what they want.

– Thanks Marcos Vinícius. I'll be watching. "I and my companions will be close by."

Marcos thanked his mentor for his help and decided to start acting.

Guided by spirituality, the boy understood that he needed to circulate a little more in society to be able to observe Paulo José's friends better. He thought for a while and called Renata again. After the greetings he said happily:

– Shall we go to the club Saturday night?

Weren't you go on a trip? – the girl asked in astonishment.

– They postponed the trip for the moment, so I'll be free for the next few days. I wanted to dance with you and feel what the energy of the music does to me. Would you like to have dinner with me?

– I accept. You can pick me up at eight. I'll be waiting for you.

After she hung up the phone Renata sat down on the sofa and, thinking about Marcos, felt how much she was in love with the boy. She remembered with pleasure the kisses they had exchanged, the emotion he aroused in her, and deep inside she felt a deep desire to stay with him forever. Overjoyed at their meeting later that night, Renata lay back on the sofa, closed her eyes, and soon fell asleep.

As the girl left the body she saw Norma, hugged her lovingly and said happily:

–How nice to see you!

– Olívia told me that you wanted to see us.

– It is true. I was feeling restless. I need to see Olavo.

– He is still under intensive treatment.

– It would not be good to visit him now. Jules has not yet authorized your visit.

– Why? I need to see him, Norma!

– To ask forgiveness for the things I have done to him. How long will I carry this sorrow in my heart?

– Everything has its time, Renata. Now, it's still impossible. Calm down.

– I want to see him, even from afar! To do something to alleviate this situation! I promise I'll restrain myself and do only what is allowed!

– Be calm! Be patient. All that will be possible, but at the right time. We must not do things on impulse. There are moments when it is necessary to act in the correct way to get what we want. Believe in the best, accept your limits and wait patiently for the right moment.

– Time is hard to pass!

– Now, you have other commitments. Calm your heart. Trust in life! If you absorb the negative energies of the world, you won't be able to achieve all the good you have come for now. After so long, life has brought you together, and you need to let the past go!

– I want to redeem myself from my past mistakes, to become a better person! – Renata insisted.

– You acted as you believed at the time. Why do you blame yourself that way? Time has passed, everything has changed, you have evolved, learned new things, developed sensitivity and today you can do great things! Forget the past and believe in the future, Renata! Life only does its best! Remember that the conquest of good is in your hands.

Renata bowed her head thoughtfully, sighed sadly and replied:

– You're right! I'll try to forget!

– Remember that mistakes teach you more than successes!

– Thank you for reminding me of that! Norma... I have come to ask your permission to go to Campos da Paz to see friends again, to feel the energies of renewal and peace there. I would also like to talk to Jules about my brother.

– I will review your request and get back to you.

At that moment, Norma came through the window. Next to her came a tall, blonde, fair-skinned girl with lively eyes, and Renata stared at her in amazement. The two girls' eyes met, and the newcomer held her gaze and smiled slightly. Norma returned:

– I want you to meet Matilde. She has been working with us for a short time. She came from another community.

– Jules holds her in high esteem! I am happy to meet her.

Matilde looked at Norma and informed her:

– We must attend to a case now! It is urgent.

Renata held Norma's hand and asked:

– I need to go to Campos da Paz to talk to Jules about my brother. I feel he needs help.

– I will give him your message.

After hugging her, Norma helped Renata return to her physical body. The girl then settled down and continued sleeping. Norma and Matilde looked around and, when they were sure that everything was calm, they went out of the window, rose in a few seconds and disappeared into infinite.

CHAPTER 6

In front of the mirror, Marcos smiled. He looked completely different than he was. Anyone who saw him would immediately imagine that he was a very rich man. He had created a humorous character of those who tell funny jokes about important people, much to the liking of Paulo José's friends. A rich young man who just wanted to enjoy everything that money could offer him. In addition, he was armed with a few provocative catchphrases in line with the boys' futile thoughts.

Marcos had spent days wondering what he would do to approach Paulo José's friends, gain their trust and make them admire him in such a way that they would eventually invite him to join the group.

Guided by spirituality, the young man decided to put his plan to work that very night. It was a Friday, and Marcos had the night off. He had arranged to go out with Renata on Saturday, because the girl would accompany her mother to a dinner party on Friday. On Fridays, Paulo José liked to gather his friends at the club and to be fondled by the girls who vied for their company.

It was after nine o'clock when Marcos, in character, entered the club. He had reserved a table and had arranged with a friend, who worked as a reporter, that later when the club was in full swing, he would approach him pretending to be doing an interview, calling everyone's attention, as if Marcos were a famous figure. They would create a scene and hope that Paulo José's group would fall for it.

Marcos entered, was led to his table and immediately sat down naturally. He noticed that Paulo José's group occupied two tables next to his and were chatting animatedly with some girls.

Discreetly observing the group, Marcos felt that he had caught the attention of Paulo José's friends, after all, in these environments, everyone practically knew each other, and any new element aroused curiosity. Would it a new rich person? Was it someone from the outside? The waiter approached him, and Marcos took the wine list in his hands and ordered. He noticed that Paulo José and two more of his friends were staring at him curiously.

Half an hour later, when the reporter arrived accompanied by a photographer to interview him, Paulo José's group fixed on him, curious and anxious to find out who this story–worthy personality was.

Marcos talked to the journalist for some time and after allowing himself to be photographed from different angles, he ended the interview.

Marcos noticed that Oscar, one of the boys from Paulo José's group of friends, had come out behind the reporter. Bluntly the boy asked:

– Who is that man you interviewed?

– He is an important lawyer, very well known. That man has worked on some impossible cases and gained fame for it.

– A famous lawyer? Wow!

– Yes, and with books published abroad. His name is Marcos.

– I'm curious! I've never heard of him.

– No?! You need to inform yourself a little more, huh? Read some newspapers...

– What do you mean?

– Well, I must go. I need to organize the interview, write the story and pass it on to the editor.

– Where will the interview be published?

– Bye, bye. I need to go!

Indecisive, Oscar shook his head, said goodbye and went to his friends. Being a vain man Oscar could not admit that he did not know things. If the reporter said that this Marcos was someone important, then he must be. He posed as a great wise man; an up–to–date figure and he did not like to be underestimated.

Oscar returned to the table where the group was and sat down, while the others stared at him curiously:

– And then? – asked Julio.

He repeated what he had heard and continued:

– He is alone. I will invite him to have some wine with us.

– Just do it. Bring him to our table, agreed Julio.

Oscar approached Marcos, handed him a card and said:

– Meeting you here tonight was a very pleasant surprise! We have been following your success and wish to get to know you better. Would a lawyer of your stature care to join us for wine?

Marcos stared at him and answered:

– Thanks for the invitation, but I prefer to stay alone at the moment.

– Why? Are you waiting for someone?

– No. I just like to be in the among people, observe them, to learn how to deal with them. Have you ever noticed how in society people like to create characters and show themselves different from what they really are?

– It's true. I know you are a leading criminal lawyer, experienced, who has written successful books, you must know psychological profiles very well and would certainly have many interesting things to tell us! Come and sit with us!

Marcos thought for a moment, nodded his head, smiled and said:

– That's fine. Since you insist, I accept.

When Marcos stood up, the friends, happily, placed another chair next to the table. Oscar introduced him and the conversation flowed pleasantly and more interestingly than they had imagined.

Encouraged by them, Marcos easily, told them about cases whose results were picturesque, leading them to laughter and a mischievous conversation much to the liking of the listeners, who clapped their hands with pleasure. Inebriated, the boys wanted to include him in the group, which meant that the first part of his plan had worked.

✱ ✱ ✱

Each day, Marcos felt more and more in love with the girl and the idea of asking her to marry him kept running through his mind. What would Renata do when she found out that he was investigating Paulo José's friends? Would she think that the boy had only approached her for information? He felt that it was time to talk to his girlfriend about the matter.

In the conversations that Marcos had with Dionísio, Renata's father sustained the thesis that the cause of the attempt against Paulo José was motivated by revenge and that the criminal was probably dangerous. Dionísio was an important criminalist, he had already sent many men to jail, and nothing could move him from the idea that his son was the victim of revenge.

During one of these conversations with Dionísio, Marcos thought for a while and considered:

– Doctor, this case seems to me different from the others. When someone wishes to take revenge for having been harmed, they usually take revenge on the person responsible for the harm. I ask myself: why instead of killing the perpetrator, the criminal chose to kill someone innocent, Doctor Dionísio? It does not make much sense to me.

– To hit me, to tear me apart, to end my life. Is there anything more painful for a father than to lose a son, Marcos? You'll be a father one day and you'll understand what I'm telling right now. This was orchestrated to shake me, to destroy me. I don't see any other way. Besides, Paulo José has no enemies. He is an educated young man he has always been respected in society, never getting involved in fights or arguments. For me the cause of the attempt is very clear.

Marcos, on the other hand, disagreed intimately with Dionísio and was still suspicious of one of Paulo José's friends. He decided to investigate further.

✵ ✵ ✵

That Saturday afternoon Estela went to visit Renata. She knew she was dating Marcos; she had already seen them together and, at a certain moment, she commented happily:

– Yesterday I went to the club and Marcos was there with Paulo José's friends! Did you know that he is the greatest joke teller? He was the only one who talked, and everyone laughed non–stop! I didn't know he had that side!

Renata was surprised that Marcos had never shown this jocular side to her before. Besides, the girl did not even know that Marcos knew her brother and his friends.

That night when Marcos came to pick her up as agreed, Renata asked:

– Why did you never tell me that you knew my brother and his friends?

Marcos stopped the car, fixed her and decided:

– That is a subject that has been worrying me. We need to talk.

Marcos took Renata to the club and chose a private place where they could talk calmly. Once seated, Renata observed that the boy was serious and waited anxiously for him to speak.

– First you will promise me that no matter what happens, you will never tell anyone what I am about to tell you. If you know anything new about me, anything at all, talk to me first.

– I promise. You can trust me.

– It's about the attempt on your brother. Renata, I work at the Federal Police with a great friend of your father's, Dr. Ignácio. We don't work directly together, but we have developed a friendship. As I have a degree in journalism and I am interested in the investigative line of work, Dr. Ignácio began to discuss some cases with me, even to experiment a new way of looking at things. That is how I started to help him unofficially in one or another job. I do that to keep my mind working.

– Are you investigating my brother's case? What do you mean? I don't understand. Where do I fit into this story?!

– Calm down. Listen to me, please. Your father went to ask Dr. Ignácio for help in investigating the case in parallel with the police, and that's how I got involved in the story. Dr.

Ignácio called me, explained the situation, and given the complexity of the problem, included me in the investigation. I want you to know however, that the fact that I met you that night had nothing to do with this. It was by chance, although I am sure that there is no such thing as chance in this life.

– Be honest with me, Marcos.

– I am being. These stories just happen to intersect. I eventually found out that you were Dr. Dionísio's daughter, but I couldn't let the investigation go because I had committed myself to helping Dr. Ignácio. Your father is aware of everything.

– Did you and my father know each other then?

– In a way, yes. We ended up getting to know each other through Dr. Ignácio.

– I get it... or I think I do. Well... I'm glad you have told me that now. I would be disappointed if you kept something so important from me for a long time.

– I wanted to protect you because I still don't know what we are dealing with, Renata. Your brother maintains that he was the victim of a robbery, but, as you know, the criminal didn't take anything of value from him. Your father believes that the attack was motivated by vendetta against him, since Dr. Dionísio is known to have put many dangerous people in jail. I am not convinced of either of these hypotheses.

– I also did not believe Paulo José's version of the attack. To me he is lying to us and to the delegate. I believe he is trying to protect one of his friends. One of them may have done something serious and he is covering it up. Unfortunately, Paulo is very tolerant and is always holding his friend's heads in his hands.

– I share the same theory. I believe that this attempt is related to one of Paulo José's friends. Something strongly points to this. Renata, how relieved I am to have told you that I am working on this case! This subject was bothering me.

– I'd like you to tell me a little more about all this, after all, I'm getting to know another Marcos, am I not?

– Well, when Dr. Ignácio invites me to participate unofficially in a case and asks me to do some investigations, I usually create characters to circulate among the suspects and be part of the group they belong, to mingle and...

– What do you mean?

– I create characters and act them out as needed. In Paulo José's case, I introduced myself to your brother and his friends as a famous lawyer. I set up a scene here with a reporter friend as if he were interviewing me to get the attention of your brother and his group. And it worked. I presented myself as a very cheerful man, who tells bad jokes the way they like them. I think they didn't want to get too deep into the questions about me because they were too embarrassed to admit they didn't know "someone so influential." They pretended to know me, but I think my jokes had more effect on them than necessarily the whole I'm someone important thing.

– I get it. And what conclusion did you come to from being around them?

– In analyzing your brother's friends, I noticed that some of them are not trustworthy, Renata. I had to get to know them better in order to know the truth about each one.

– Have you ever worked in theater?

– No, but when I was a teenager, I liked to create characters and do plays. My sister and my younger brother helped me. I wrote the play; my sister and my younger brother were the actors. I would invite the kids and the price of admission was ten matchsticks.

Marcos kissed Renata's hand affectionately and continued:

– This was a very good time! I felt so much pleasure in doing theater that when I developed mediumship and began to work with spirituality, I thought of using that experience for the greater good. The spirits who help me even suggest ideas to collaborate with me. Imagination is a useful tool for life!

– So, don't you do this work for money? Isn't my father paying for this research? All of this is still a little foggy for me.

– Of course not, Renata. As I told you I go into these investigations for two reasons: first, because it's a way to help spirituality; second, because I have a degree in journalism, I've always been fascinated by the investigative line of work. It was the way I found to do something I like, even without working directly with it and keep my mind working. Or maybe I'm an inveterate fan of Sherlock Holmes stories and want to one day to publish my own as well!

Renata smiled more calmly, kissed Marcus and commented:

– Paulo José's case has not yet been clarified. Although he is being watched by two security guards hired by my father, I feel that this is not enough. I am sure that he is in danger precisely because the danger is close to him. I feel that my brother lied to the delegate.

– I think so too. It's really hard to convince your father that the threat is close to your brother and not far away. He still thinks that the attack was committed by a thug and that this man will come back to finish what he started.

– Do you think my brother is still in this danger?

– Yes, my love. Yes. That shot was fired to kill your brother. The criminal must be waiting for time to pass and for the case to be forgotten. We must continue to protect him. We can't make it easy!

Renata was silent for a few seconds, frowned and said:

– Marcos, I just remembered something that happened the night of my parents' party...

– What did you remember?

– I don't know if this has anything to do with the attack, but since you are investigating the case, I guess you should know?

– Talk just like that.

– The night was beautiful that day, and I went to the garden to admire it. I then sat down on a bench to rest, and, after a few minutes, I heard a woman's voice speaking very angrily: "You can't do that with me! What am I going to do with my life now? You're going to have to marry me! If my father finds out, you won't come out of this story alive!" Frightened, I got up to leave, looked around and saw that I would have to pass by them, so I decided to wait. I sat down again and heard a male voice, saying angrily, "I never promised you anything and I won't marry you. I can't, you know that. I can't afford to get married now! You gave yourself up because you wanted to. I never forced you." The girl replied: "You never forced me, but you accepted my love and now you want to get rid of it! Be careful, because I am desperate! You don't know what I'm capable of. In fact, you don't know what a desperate woman is capable of!"

– And what else did you hear? – Marcos asked.

– The man said: "I never promised to marry you and I'm not going to marry you!" The girl was furious and replied: "I'm pregnant! You must marry me! You can't do that!" He was once again rude to her and said: "Never! You gave yourself up because you wanted to!"

– And what did the girl response when he told her that?

– She said: "You bastard! Right now, I am going into that room and tell everything. I'll make a fuss! I want to see where your reputation as a good guy will ends!" The boy, then, finished by saying: "Do this and everyone will have a good time at your expense! I'm not the fool you think I am!

– And after that? What happened? – Marcos was attentive to the details of what Renata was telling him.

– She turned her back and walked into the room and I was terrified. It was my parents' party, and such a scandal would be very unpleasant. I immediately went back to the room, called my friend Estela and invited her to circulate around the party. I did that to try to find someone among the guests whose features had changed. Something to suggested that they had just gotten out of an argument. I tried hard to identify the girl but could not. Had she left?

– And the next morning, Paulo José suffered the attack. Was that it?

– Do you think that what I told you has to do with the attack?

– A woman who is hurt and pregnant is capable of anything.

Renata thought for a while and said:

– My brother likes the social life but so far, he hasn't had any steady girlfriend. I don't know, Marcos. Maybe the attack has nothing to do with what I told you.

Marcos was silent for a few seconds and answered:

– It's a clue. I'll see how far it goes.

– I think the girl made a vague, outspoken threat but she didn't have the courage to do what she promised. She was hurt and angry, after all, she would have to face her family because of the pregnancy. But I don't think she took it that further.

Marcos hugged Renata, lightly kissed the girl's cheek and said seriously:

– I loved how you solved the case and protected yourself from scandal. Have you heard anything else?

– Unfortunately, no. I looked for her, but I couldn't identify who it was.

– Maybe she's not even in your brother's group. Maybe she has even infiltrated the party with the intention of pressuring the boy.

Renata thought for a while and then said:

– She seemed to be pretty, classy, but she may have really gone undercover. She intended to make a scandal of pressuring him! I became very afraid that she would do what she promised. I went into the room to look for her, but I couldn't find her.

– And the boy, did you find him?

– He was on his back. I couldn't see his face. Anyway, Marcos, I don't think that this argument was the cause of the attack on my brother's life. I have observed that Paulo has been very tolerant with his friends. I would be relieved if he cut off friendship with at least two.

– It would be better if he cut more than that.

– Unfortunately, my brother is very tolerant and keeps grabbing his friend's heads. Sometimes Paulo is even amused when some of them do bad things, saying that they are still in their infancy and need to grow up. He does not teach them or demand that they learn to become better people. I really wish that, after what happened, my brother would pay more attention to his friends' behavior.

– You are right. The case has not been solved yet and, after all, there were two shots! I heard from Dr. Ignácio that the delegate believes in the hypothesis of revenge and that I want the criminal to take a break. And, when he thinks that everything is calm, he will come back to finish what he started.

Renata stared at him and said seriously:

– I still think that Paulo José lied to the delegate when he talked about the attack. Something is still not clear about what happened. Is my brother trying to protect one of his friends?

– Why would your brother lie? Would he be able to protect someone who had assaulted him? I don't think so. The shot was meant to kill, which makes us think that the person who fired the shot was very angry. I am not sure if it was one of Paulo's friends who made the shot, you know? Maybe one of them got into trouble, and your brother, protecting him, left someone angry.

– What do you mean?

– I have friends who often show me things. Things that I need to see. Marcos Vinícius is one of them! He teaches me that God is at the helm of everything.

– What is he like?

– A little shorter than me, with light skin, brown hair and honey-colored eyes, which as his emotions turn greenish. He is always upbeat and makes jokes about everything. Those who don't know him believe he is lazy and underestimate his strength, but when he needs to act, he is very lucid, firm, dominates the situation, and gets everything he wants.

– I would like to meet him.

– We talked about the case, and he is present now. Concentrate and try to make contact.

Renata closed her eyes and said in thought: "I would very much like to meet you!"

Renata's lips opened in a pleasant smile, and then she stared at Marcos and said happily:

– Besides handsome, he is very elegant and gentle.

– You really saw him! That is just the way he is.

– He bowed, looked at me with affection, and I felt a great sense of well-being.

– Marcos Vinícius usually acts like this when he likes someone.

– I feel he will help us protect my brother.

– Yes, he will help us find out what is behind the attack.

While analyzing the case, Marcos felt that there was something more to the story. Deep inside, he was certain that Paulo José lied, and that the boy seemed to be in a hurry to explain to the delegate that the motive for the attack was an attempted robbery.

– He is fine now – Marcos tried to calm Renata down.

The girl thought for a while and then said:

– I feel that the danger has not yet passed.

– Do you suspect anyone?

– Even if I think that this story has to do with his friends, I would not allow Oscar, Horácio and João in the house anymore. I feel they are not trustworthy. I have the feeling that they are always acting. They are too helpful; they are always praising Paulo José and do everything to please him. This exaggeration sometimes makes me feel uncomfortable.

– You are very observant and have great sensitivity, Renata. Keep watching them and, if you notice anything suspicious, don't do anything, because it could be dangerous. Talk to me. I will know what to do without them noticing.

Renata sighed and said seriously:

– Whoever attacked him intended to kill, but since he couldn't, he must return to finish what he started.

– The two men who are protecting your brother are experienced, they know what they are doing.

– For now, but I would like this case to be settled once and for all so that we can be at peace. We can't spend the rest of our lives under this threat!

– You are right. For now, everything is under control. Stay calm. Nothing bad will happen to your brother. I'm sure everything will be cleared up and the culprits will be caught. You can wait!

– I believe you! It's late. It's time for us to go home.

Shortly afterwards, Marcos' car drove into the garden and stopped in front of the front door. Marcos hugged Renata affectionately and kissed her several times. The girl sighed and said softly:

– It's late. I need to get in!

– Every day it gets harder and harder to separate myself from you! Renata... will you marry me? I know it seems too soon, I know it seems like a crazy act on my part, but I feel in my heart that you are the woman of my life. All of it. Why, then, wait any longer? If you accept my request, I'll talk to your father tomorrow. What do you think?

Caught by surprise, Renata smile with bright eyes answered:

– This might be a good option – intimately, she also felt that she had a deep and special connection with Marcos.

The couple kissed once more, and Renata said happily:

– Tomorrow we will talk about the details.

The two kissed once more and Renata went home feeling a strong emotion and great well-being in her heart. More than in love, the girl felt that the bonds she had with Marcos were of a deep, mature love that came from many lives.

CHAPTER 7

Dionísio was sitting in his office when the secretary came in and told him:

– Mr. Marcos has arrived. Can he come in?

– Yes. And as long as he's here, I'm not for anyone.

– Yes, sir.

Dionísio stood up and hugged Marcos, saying:

– I hope you have good news! Sit down.

Marcos stared at him seriously and then said:

– The first thing I must tell you, Mr. Dionísio, is that Renata and I love each other, we are dating and that I have asked her to marry me. Would you accept me in your family?

Surprised, Dionísio looked at him and answered:

– My boy, although I am surprised, after all, this is a recent flirtation, I have admiration and respect for you, and I know that Renata is an intelligent, loving and correct girl. There are dates and engagements that go on for years, but are not underpinned by sincere love, and I don't see that in you. In my heart, I believe that you really love each other and that you have everything to build a beautiful life together.

– Thank you very much for your words, Mr. Dionísio. I am not rich, but I have possibilities to offer Renata a comfortable life. When we met, we felt that we already knew each other from other lives. You know that both she and I are spiritualists, we believe that the spirit is eternal, and that life continues after death. We have never talked about this subject, but I would like to know your opinion.

– Since childhood, Renata has claimed to see spirits, to talk to them and, has often given me proof that she was telling the truth. From a very early age she said profoundly true things. Things that are out of line with what is expected for her age. I would like to have that certainty. I would like to have the certainty that my daughter has, but sometimes, when facing death, knowing that my body or the bodies of the people I love will be destroyed by worms, I feel insecure, and I don't like to think about it. I don't understand how a child can speak naturally about death, saying that everything is right and that the best always happens, but I have learned to live with this.

– Believing in eternity brings calm and joy of life. Our true home is in the astral world, Mr. Dionísio. During the day we are in the world, but at night, we return to our home of origin to rebuild our energies. Think about this and do not be afraid to go deeper into this knowledge. It is not difficult. Try it and you will see.

– If we are eternal, why do we need to be born into this world, to live in a perishable body of flesh, that gets sick with time and dies? To me, that is very cruel!

Mark stared at him seriously and answered calmly:

– Everything that God does has a reason for being. He, with his immense wisdom, created our planet, the Earth, where time is slower compared to that of the astral world. Therefore, living here, we can learn more easily how life works, which favors knowledge. Even reincarnated, the spirit can analyze its attitudes and change its behavior to build a better life. There are moments when the spirit realizes that it needs to evolve more to be happier, recognizes where it has been deluded, and makes an effort to change. Who can know what goes on in someone's head at the hour of death?

– Dionísio stared at Marcos and said seriously:

– Just thinking about it gave me a chill. It's better to change the subject. You are young! You should be interested in living and enjoying your youth. Everything goes by so fast and, when we wake up, the opportunities will be gone.

Marcos smiled and answered:

– Mr. Dionísio, your daughter and I are Spiritualists, and we want to enjoy our stay on Earth. We try to be true in our attitudes and this is the best way. Life has secrets, but it is very rich and always tries to offer us the best, even if we are reincarnated. The important thing is to know the truth, to discover how things work and to ennoble good results, always working honestly and well with life. I would like to know if you accept me as your son–in–law.

Dionísio thought for a while and decided to ask Marcos a question:

– Did she know you would talk to me about this subject?

– Yes. Last night, we talked seriously about our future and decided to get married when possible. Although I had scheduled this meeting with you to deal with your son's case, I was anxious to know if you would accept me into your family. I truly love Renata and I am certain that our spirits must walk together on this journey in order to develop our potentials.

– I am happy that Renata has chosen you, my boy. I feel that this marriage will work out very well.

– I am sure of it. Our love is old! I felt it since I first saw her.

Thoughtfully, Dionísio stared at Marcos and commented:

– To love and be loved is something that makes our lives so much better. After thirty years of marriage, my relationship with Eunice has grown stronger. We still love and understand each other very well. She is much better than I am. I confess that she understands me without me having to say anything. I am sure that the same thing will happen to you.

Marcos commented:

– Well, now we need to talk about the attack.

– Have you found out anything else?

– We have no proof yet, but I feel that Paulo José is facing something very serious.

– Why do you think this, Marcos? My son is always well, he knows how to lead a life. The attack he suffered was to hurt me. I am almost certain that it was one of the henchmen of some dangerous bandit that I helped put in jail.

– I have my doubts, Mr. Dionísio. According to Renata, Paulo José has been keeping quiet about the attack, even though he knows that the murderer may be waiting for the right occasion to attack him again. Don't you find this very suspicious? Someone being attacked and wanting to close the case, even without a solution? I feel he is not telling everything he knows.

– My son has never been involved in anything dangerous, Marcos. He is an educated boy, who wants to live life and have fun with his friends. Who would have any reason to try to kill him? None of this makes any sense to me.

Marcos thought for a while and asked:

– Is he protecting someone?

Dionísio looked at Marcos seriously and exclaimed:

– I don't think so. He almost died!

– Paulo is very tolerant with friends, but I will find out the truth. I have already won the group's trust and, little by little, always with discretion, I will be able to obtain more information about the boys' daily lives. And with a little bit of luck, the truth will emerge. No secret remains hidden when life decides to teach us its precious lessons. I am confident.

– Were you able to find out anything?

– I noticed that they like heavy jokes, badmouthing people in society and are suspicious. I joined in, used the same language, and they started to open.

Dionísio frowned and commented:

– I did not know that my son got involved with people like that. Renata had already warned me that Paulo José should be more careful with his friendships and about bringing certain people into the house. I thought she was exaggerating.

– You can be sure that she has not exaggerated. I made a list of the closest friends, the ones who are always with Paulo José, and their environment is not the best.

Dionísio thought for a while and then asked:

– Do you think that one of them might have been the mastermind of the attack?

– This point is not yet clear, but the time of truth is coming. We just need to believe and have faith in the designs of spirituality.

– I will talk to Paulo about this possibility.

– Wait a little longer. Renata told me about something that happened the night of your party.

– What? She didn't tell me anything. What happened?

In a few words, Marcos related what Renata had told him and finished:

– Renata told me what she witnessed that night. She could not see the couple, but she heard their unpleasant conversation. The girl was pregnant and wanted the boy to assume the supposed child. He, however, treated her badly and said he would never marry her, which made her furious. She said she would go to the party hall and tell everyone what was going on. Worried about the scandal, Renata ran to the hall willing to stop her in every way, but everything was calm, and her daughter concluded that the girl had left the party.

– I believe that this has nothing to do with the attack, Marcos. In society these things are common. Many girls give a belly blow to get a rich husband; and others, who have money and an important family, go to the doctor to "solve the problem."

Marcos stared at the future father-in-law for a few seconds and replied:

– A woman betrayed and scorned can be dangerous, Mr. Dionísio. Regardless of who the boy is, he has acted arbitrarily, without considering the girl's feelings. Sooner or later, he will have to bear the consequences of his bad choices.

Dionísio shook his head and smiled as he said:

– They are like many dogs that bark, but do not bite. They complain, they put themselves as victims, but do not have the courage to do anything. I still maintain the hypothesis that the attack is related to some criminal I put in jail, and I am suspicious of the last case I caught. That is the right clue. Don't waste time investigating stories that will lead you nowhere, Marcos, because you will only have a headache.

Even though he did not agree with Dionísio's mistaken judgment of women, Marcos considered:

– Okay. I will keep investigating. When I have something new, we'll talk again.

Despite Dionísio's position, Marcos felt like going deeper into the story Renata had told him. Who, after all, was the girl who treated the pregnant girl with such disregard? How would she have reacted to that situation? If only he knew who the girl was, maybe he could find out more.

Perhaps Renata remembered some detail that could identify the girl, something that at that moment, had gone unnoticed, but that would come back to her memory if she made the effort.

As soon as he left Dionísio's office, Marcos called his girlfriend's house.

– I need to talk to you. Would you agree to have dinner with me tonight?

– I wasn't thinking of leaving home. Wouldn't it be better if you came here for dinner?

– It's about the attempt on your brother's life. The subject is confidential. I'd like to hear your opinion.

– Okay. What time are you coming?

– At eight o'clock sharp I'll be there. I can't wait to meet you.

– I'll be looking forward to it.

✳ ✳ ✳

A few minutes before the appointed time, Marcos arrived, and Renata went to receive him. He hugged her and kissed her gently on the cheek. Then, eye to eye, he said, moved:

– With each passing day that passes, I feel more and more like being with you. My love grows every day, and your presence has become a light in my life. Today, I can't imagine going on without the lucidity that your eyes offer me. You are my companion on my journey. I am sure that life has united us for a greater purpose.

– I miss you too. I have always dreamed of someone who would understand me and allow me to express my feelings freely. With you Marcos, I feel secure enough and to face any obstacle life imposes on me.

After a passionate kiss, Marcos explained:

– Shall we set a date for our wedding? I talked to your father about us. I proposed and he accepted, but he said that first I must solve the case of the attempt. He is afraid that the assassin will strike again, and that the rest of the family will also be affected.

– Do you think this is possible?

– Everything is possible, my love. Whoever fired the shot intended to kill and may come back. It is better that we talk about this matter outside of here, because the walls have ears. In these cases, we need to be careful. You never know what might happen.

Renata agreed, and they went to a restaurant. They sat down in a discreet place, where they could talk without reservation. As soon as they were settled, Marcos said seriously:

– I have been thinking a lot about the case of that girl who was pregnant. About that argument you heard during your parents' party.

– Do you really think that this issue could have something to do with the attack?

– In an investigation, we can't miss any details. She threatened him that she would make a scandal, but she didn't follow through on the threat, which doesn't mean she forgot about it. She might just be waiting for the right moment to act.

– Do you think so?

– It's a hypothesis. Don't you remember any details about the girl? Think for a moment. Maybe you saw something that you didn't notice at the time?

– From what I saw, she was an elegant girl. She was certainly someone from high society.

– Think, make an effort. Any detail is very important. I'd like to follow this lead as well.

Renata thought for a while and finally said:

– I couldn't see the couple properly, my love, as it was too dark. Besides, I didn't want them to notice my presence. Now, however, on second thought I may have seen a light brown hair and a blue dress or a black one. I am not sure. The girl was very nervous and threatened to cause a scandal, if the boy did not marry her.

– Didn't you see anyone with these characteristics after the party?

– No. You know... I don't go to the club very often.

– You're a member of the club, aren't you?

– My dad bought a club membership and my whole family can attend it. Paulo enjoys it the most. He's made many friends there and is always at the club.

– Are all your brother's friends' members of the club?

– No. Besides Paulo, only three of them are members and can bring friends as guests.

Renata was thoughtful for a few seconds and then said:

– Marcos, Dad is very experienced and believes that the cause of the attack was revenge because he put a very dangerous criminal in jail. Doesn't this sound like a more plausible motive?

– I intend to investigate both sides, but I know that a betrayed woman is capable of anything. In the cases I have studied, this has been more common than it seems. I will find out the truth.

– Dad fears the killer will return to finish what he started. Our family could be in danger. This feels like a nightmare. I have asked for the help of my spiritual friends to resolve this situation as soon as possible.

– I heard from Dr. Ignacio that there are some policemen watching Paulo José.

– Will they find any clues?

– No. In addition to the policemen who are investigating the case, your father continues to keep a private surveillance to protect them. He believes that the criminal is giving some time to make us think that he gave up his attempt.

– Dad will not rest until he finds out who did this to my brother. Every week, he talks to the delegate to see if they have found any clues, but so far, they have found nothing.

– He fears that something will happen to either of you. It is important that your brother cooperates.

– Paulo usually doesn't take things too seriously, but after what he has been through, he will certainly follow Dad's orders.

Marcos smiled and said happily:

– Now, let's talk about us! Yesterday, walking through my neighborhood, I saw a beautiful house for sale. It was open to visitors, but I didn't go inside. I'd like you to come with me to see it. If you like it, maybe I can buy it.

– We can go tomorrow! I'd love to! What time are you coming home?

– I'll be working in the morning, but I can pick you up at 1:00. Is that okay?

– I'm curious to see the house. Have you been to visit it yet?

– No. I just walked by and talked to the realtor. He was just finishing opening the house for a visitation. I will call the realtor tomorrow morning and schedule an appointment in the afternoon for a visit. The place is nice, my neighborhood is good, the house is old, but very well built in the middle of the land. It even has a beautiful garden.

– I am looking forward to seeing it. I am sure that our future home will be built with a lot of love and understanding.

– I am also very happy about our marriage. We will be very happy.

Renata smiled, and the girl's eyes sparkled when she said:

– I like old houses, with high ceilings and a beautiful garden surrounding the property. If we close the deal, I want to dedicate myself to decorating. I will use neutral tones and decorate the house with great taste. We will receive friends, and, in the springtime, we will gather the family to enjoy the blooming garden.

– I forgot to tell you that the house has a beautiful, large and well-ventilated balcony.

Renata put her arms around Marcos' neck, and their lips met. They kissed several times, and he said excitedly:

– You are the woman of my life! As soon as I saw you, I felt it! We will be very happy, my love! I'm sure of it! When love is true, life flows with prosperity.

Excited, Renata and Marcos kept making plans for the future until the girl looked at the watch and said:

– It's time to go! It's late. You have an appointment early tomorrow morning.

– We are taking care of our future! Everything is going to work out fine.

– I know it will.

When Marcos arrived at Renata's house, Marcos kissed the girl passionately. They were full of plans for the future and anxious not to have to say goodbye anymore. Renata drove home convinced that she had found true love and was happy, and while driving home, Marcos thought about the moment that the girl would become his wife.

CHAPTER 8

It was a little after two o'clock in the afternoon when Dionísio arrived at his office. He hurried to his office. He had arrived early with the intention of studying a case, the hearing of which was scheduled for two days later. Janete, the secretary, had already placed the case on the lawyer's desk, and he sat down ready to start working. However, the secretary knocked lightly on the door before entering and said:

– Excuse me, doctor.

– What is it?

– Sorry to bother you, Doctor Dionísio, but a couple says they have an urgent need to speak with you.

– Are they, my clients?

– No.

– I'm only available by appointment only. Besides, I'm busy. Ask them to make an appointment and come back another day.

– Doctor Dionísio, I told them that, but they insisted on talking to you. They say they urgently need your help and that they will not leave without talking to you.

– I don't like to be pressured.

– They are middle-aged people and seem very nervous.

Dionísio thought for a while and then said:

– I can see that I will not be able to do what I want to do! Send them in.

Dionísio put the file in the drawer, stood up and waited for the people to come in. After greeting them, he asked them to sit in front of his desk, looked at them and asked:

– How can I help you?

The man took a photograph out of his pocket and handed it to Dionísio saying:

– Our daughter has been missing for more than a month, doctor Dionísio. We are in a very difficult situation. We have looked for the police, who have been working on the case, but no one has found anything so far. It's been more than a month! Earlier today, I looked for the delegate and I didn't like what I heard.

– What did he tell you?

– "You should not worry. We're sure that she'll soon show up! You know how today's young girls are! They fall in love, get deluded and run away from home. Isn't it what happened?"

João Alberto, that is what the man was called, shook his head and continued nervously:

– My daughter is a serious girl, who has always behaved well! She would never do that! She didn't take any personal belongings. Her clothes are all there. We are very distressed. We have come to look for you in the hope that you will find out what is really going on!

The man took a card from his pocket and handed it to Dionísio:

– This is my business card.

Dionisio took the card and read: João Alberto Fiorucci.

– You know that I am a lawyer, don't you, sir? Who does not act actively in investigations.

– Yes, Doctor Dionísio, I know that. I know this is not your role, but you are an important criminalist, you have worked on many cases, and you can help us think of possibilities. The police are trying to find answers to my daughter's disappearance, but I feel that nothing is moving forward. Help us! In addition, we have a lot of admiration for you for putting in jail the man who killed Dr. Vilela. He was our friend. He was a good man, polite, treated everyone with respect.

– What I can promise you is to get in touch with some people who have experience with crime investigation.

– We don't know what to do anymore. We came here because we are desperate. We went to practically all the hospitals in the city and nearby towns, the Institute of Forensic Medicine, and we found nothing. Emilia is not satisfied. We are very distressed, that's why we came to look for you. We trust you, and I am sure you will find out what happened.

Emilia laid her hand on Dionísio's, and there were tears in her eyes when she said:

– Please, doctor, help us! I feel that something very serious has happened to her! Marlene is a proper girl, she graduated in psychology last year. She is a studious and responsible girl. She never repeated a year. I feel that something very bad happened to her! In this world there are some very evil people... We came to look for you, because we are confident that you can find her!

João Alberto said in distress:

– I feel that she is alive! And I know that you will help us find out where she is!

– You are our last hope! – Emilia reinforced.

Dionísio looked at the couple with compassion. He was also a father and sympathized with the affliction of Marlene's parents.

– I also have children and I understand the gravity of the moment they are going through. As I told you, as a lawyer, I do not work directly in investigations, but I know good professionals who will be able to work in parallel with the police.

– We are willing to spend whatever it takes to do this. We trust in you, and we know that it was God who brought us here. You are the only one capable of finding our beloved daughter. Your competence is unquestionable.

– Mr. Fiorucci, can I hire the staff?

– Yes, doctor. I have complete confidence in the choice of professionals. I'm willing to spend my last penny until I find my daughter.

– All right. I would like you to write down all the information you consider relevant about Marlene. If you have any photographs of the girl, please leave them with me.

– Of course! We have some photos here, said João Alberto.

Dionisio handed them paper and pencil and made some recommendations:

– I ask both of you to make your notes, because what one doesn't remember to quote, the other will certainly remember. I need her full name, routine, friends' names and other details that may help locate her. Write down your phone number.

While the couple wrote, trying hard to give useful information to the lawyer, Dionísio watched them, thinking that most likely the girl was happy with a boyfriend and that, after a while, she would return home ashamed. Then, the parents would immediately arrange the wedding to save the girl's honor. It was an easy case to solve.

Dionísio reflected on the difficulties of life and the wrong choices some people made. Without realizing the abyss into which the human being, trapped by the illusions of the world, plunges, he follows tortuous paths and attracts unnecessary afflictions.

Marlene's parents, attentive not to forget any detail, wrote down on paper everything they considered important about their daughter, about the girl's relationship with her family, her friends and the routine that Marlene had. João Alberto finished his notes before his wife did and, still stunned, reviewed the two sheets of paper they had written.

Then handed them to Dionísio, who began to read avidly, while Emilia continued writing.

João Alberto described the daughter as a very correct girl, affectionate with her parents and loved by all. Dionísio, however, knew that parents always see their children as having more qualities than they really have, and that they usually do not see their defects. The lawyer had full conviction that the case was easy to solve. He was experienced and knew how to act in that situation. With João Alberto's agreement, he would hire a good private investigator, distribute photos of Marlene to all the police stations, and the girl would soon be located.

When Emilia handed over her notes, Dionísio put them in a folder along with João Alberto's, who without further ado begged:

– The case is serious, doctor Dionísio, help us find our daughter!

– That is what I will do.

– I want to follow up on all the details. Anything you discover, let me know without delay. Our daughter is our most precious asset. The family has been destroyed since she disappeared.

Emilia fixed her eyes on Dionísio and very moved, said:

– I will continue to pray that nothing bad happens to my daughter. She is not used to going out alone. She is a good, loving and very kind girl!

– Rest assured. I already know who I can hire to investigate the case.

João Alberto took a checkbook out of his pocket, filled out a sheet and handed it to Dionísio, saying:

I hope this amount will cover the first expenses. Keep us informed, Doctor Dionísio. We are stressed, with fear of what might have happened to our daughter. We will know how to reward you very well. Marlene is our angel! If something happens to her, we will have no more will to live!

– I will do what you ask. I know how difficult a situation like that is!

After Marlene's parents said goodbye, Dionísio sat down again and reread the information the couple had written down.

Sometime later, Dionísio, distracted, did not even hear a knock at the door. He awoke when he heard a familiar voice:

– May I come in?

Dionísio stood up smiling:

– You came at the right time! But, first, tell me: did you find out anything about the attack?

– Mr. Dionísio, I have some suspects, however, I still don't have any evidence to point to the right person. Why did I arrive at the right time?

– A couple came to me for help. Their only daughter has disappeared, and they are desperate, thinking the worst. I will send a copy of the girl's photo to all police stations. The parents claim that she is a good girl, loved by all and very wise and they fear that the girl has been a victim of evil. I did not take the case too seriously though. They said she doesn't have a boyfriend but who knows! Nowadays, young girls just do what they want and don't listen to their parents. She might have run away with the boyfriend, given herself to him and now she is ashamed to come back home.

Marcos faced the future father-in-law, thought for a while and pronounced in a firm voice:

– You are wrong. The girl's parents are right. Something wrong happened to her.

– How do you know about it?

– She is a tall, very beautiful, elegant girl with light brown, slightly wavy hair, light skin and green eyes. She has good energy. She is a balanced and lucid person.

Dionísio shook his head and commented:

– How do you know all this without knowing her?

Still incredulous, the lawyer opened the drawer, took out a photo of Marlene from inside a folder and handed it to Marcos saying:

– You don't need her picture to know what she looks like, but I want you to get a good fix on the girl. Will I then be able to see the truth? Although I know that it is you who has this power, it is always good to reinforce my faith!

Seeing that Marcos stared at the picture for a few seconds, Dionísio waited with some anxiety and, as he remained silent, he asked:

– And then? What are you feeling? Did you discover something?

– I feel that she is in danger, but I am still not seeing everything clearly. I will take a copy of the notes of the girl's parents and deepen my observations. I need to consult my spiritual friends.

– Do that. They must know where she is. Then you can find out the location and solve the case.

– That's not how it works, Mr. Dionísio. The spirituality helps us, protects us, but it is not allowed to intervene directly in our lives. We have our free will and spirituality respects our individual choices.

– I don't understand! They know everything and can't help us? What is the point?

Marcos smiled and said:

– The help must be adequate. Moreover, their circumstances, their thoughts and emotions, their fears, can get mixed up and mess things up further. No one will be helped unless they respect and learn the laws that govern the universe. We are responsible for our choices, and we reap the fruits of our actions.

Dionísio reflected on what Marcos had said and asked:

– What about the attack? Have you found out anything else?

– I've been with the guys at the club. For now, I'm gaining their trust.

– Paulo José's case is more serious, Marcos. It is better that you dedicate yourself more to this. I would like you to work on the mystery that involves the disappearance of this girl, but not to leave aside the investigation of the attack that my son suffered.

– Mr. Dionísio, both cases are serious. I am working on Paulo José's case and now I will also dedicate myself to that girl, Marlene, won't I?

Dionísio shrugged his shoulders and said smugly:

– Yes, yes. Do as you wish but keep me informed about everything you find out! When I know who shot Paulo José, the person responsible will go to jail, whoever's son he is! Remember that this element was not just trying to scare my family! His goal was to murder my son!

Dionísio remained silent for a few seconds and then said confidently:

– I am almost certain that this attack did not come from a good family! I believe that whoever shot at Paulo must be from a poor family. Maybe he did it out of envy or even was paid by some criminal that I helped put in jail.

– Aren't you being prejudiced, Mr. Dionísio? Why would this attack necessarily come from a poor person? Do you really believe that a person who comes from a rich family cannot also commit atrocities? There are rich and rotten homes, and poor and full of light homes. I see no logic in that relationship.

Seriously, Dionísio answered:

– I'm just being realistic, my boy. Society is full of criminals, who only want to harm good families. We are part of a select group.

Marcos did not want to argue, because he knew that it would take time for Dionísio to understand the laws of life. Knowledge is light and awakens the spirit in all its divine capacity. It is always necessary to look at the same situation from another perspective, analyzing each new feeling, each experience, because there will always be much to learn, even if our limited vision believes to have exhausted the subject.

After the conversation with his future father-in-law, Marcos went straight home and went to a room that he kept locked and where no one else could enter. In this room the boy prayed, elevated his spirit and maintained contact with friendly spirits that helped him on his journey. They filled that space with high energies, making the place an oasis of peace and protection for Marcos.

The boy entered the room, put the papers with Marlene's parents' notes on the table and closed his eyes. Placing a hand on each sheet of paper, he connected with the spirits and waited.

A feeling of anguish overcame Marcos, who saw a wooden room lit by a dim light coming from a lantern. The boy sharpened his senses, and a very unpleasant smell of oil invaded his nose. A girl was lying on a wooden bed, but her sleep was not peaceful. She seemed to be doped up and oblivious to everything.

It was dark and Marcos could not tell if the girl was the young woman he was looking for. The scene suddenly faded, and Marcos breathed a sigh of relief.

One of the spirits assisting him said:

–I tried to enter that place and felt that it was blocked by dangerous energies that would make it difficult for me to leave later. Even with difficulty, I saw that two–armed men are sitting outside, taking over the place and willing to prevent anyone from getting close. I know how they do this and decided to ask my friends for help to defeat them. The atmosphere is very heavy.

– It's Marlene! She is desperate. How she tried to escape, they tied her to the bed. Where is this place?

–It's a plot of land far from the city, where there's a wooden house with some old furniture and no comfort.

– I need to find out the exact location.

–Do that.

Marcos thought for a while and said:

– I feel that we still can't understand this case. According to the girl's parents, she is intelligent, dignified and educated. The family is well–off, so why hasn't anyone asked for the ransom yet? Why? Could it be that she fell in love with some bad element, got involved with him and didn't tell her parents? I feel there is a mystery to this. Ask your masters for help, maybe they will give you some hints. If you find out anything let me know. I will keep trying to understand better. Did you find out anything else about the attack? – Marcos asked the spiritual friend.

–Yes, I have studied the boys. I have noticed that although Júlio continues to lead a normal life, he is nervous, he takes tranquilizers and, yet he can't calm down. He has been thinking very angrily about a girl, as if he wanted to get back at her.

– Was he the one who kidnapped Marlene?

–Yes, but he didn't do it alone. He hired people and keeps showing up here to save his own skin.

He is a bad character. No wonder I sense something bad emanating from Paulo José's group of friends. We need to act fast. I believe he is thinking about releasing her and my fear is that Marlene can't withstand the pressure.

–I also feel this way. I will hold a meeting with our comrades, we will study how we'll act, and I will come to program the action with you.

After some orientations the group said goodbye. Marcos sat down and reread the notes that Marlene's parents made and suddenly the possibility of Júlio being involved in both crimes crossed his mind. The more he thought about it, the more it made sense. In the assassination attempt, the person had shot to kill, because he was probably very angry, but there was no woman in the case. But why would Júlio shoot his friend?

For some reason, Marcos sensed that the two events were connected, but why? And if Julio was really involved in both crimes, would he have acted without the friends' knowledge or with their help?

Marcos felt that the kidnapped girl was desperate and feared the worst, so he needed to act quickly. Without wasting time, he took Marlene's photograph, stared at it and mentally connected with her, saying affectionately:

– Marlene, my name is Marcos, and I am working to free you! I am collaborating with the police, and soon we will find out where you are. Stay strong, pray and ask for God's help because He is protecting you. Trust that soon we will free you. Believe that faith moves mountains! Even when everything seems difficult and bad, in the end, what happened will be reverted into learning and knowledge. Keep peace and trust in your heart! We are together!

Although she was nervous and a little doped up, Marlene noticed that someone was trying to comfort her. Marcos continued:

– Believe what I'm telling you and stay calm, so that they don't dope you. You need to be well for us to be able to liberate you. They are dangerous, but we are stronger than they are. Trust in life and in us. Stay with God!

Marcos kept repeating the words of support and confidence until, tired, he settled down to sleep, putting the case in God's hands and his spiritual friends.

CHAPTER 9

Marcos woke up when it started to get light. He got up feeling that he needed to do something to free the girl and solve the mystery surrounding the attack on Paulo José's life, but he still had no idea what he would do.

As soon as he got into the car, Marcos asked his spiritual friends for help and felt Ernesto's presence beside him, saying:

–Marcos, I came to help you, but I must tell you that your anxiety is preventing you from finding the true path. Trust in the laws of life, for they are functional, and no one is without divine protection. Remember, however, that there are times when we must go forward and times when we must go backward. It is common sense that determines every action.

– Last night, I had the feeling that Paulo José's case and Marlene's are somehow linked. What do you think about that?

Ernesto thought for a while and answered:

–Things are not clear. I can check. Even in the spiritual world, we encounter difficulties, and we have to seek clarity. Calm your heart.

In his searches, the spirit friend realized that the case was very serious, and that Marlene was at risk of death, since

Júlio was her karma from other lives. In previous lives, the girl had been cruel and bitter to the boy, leading him to commit suicide. While there was love from the boy, the girl's indifference had transmuted that feeling into hatred. Ernesto noticed that therein lay the key to unraveling that complicated case.

In her past life, Marlene belonged to a noble family, she was very beautiful and cultured, but also overbearing and proud. Her parents, blinded by the love they nurtured for their only daughter, did not know her true character.

Inside Marlene there were two personalities – one good one and a bad one– which emerged according to the situation the girl was exposed to. If contradicted, she would become spiteful, overbearing and capable of anything, but on a day-to-day basis, she was docile and friendly with her parents, who mistakenly, did her every whim.

When Júlio and Marlene met, the boy soon fell in love with the girl, who nurtured that love as a whim. However, as time went by, she began to tire of the boy's courtship and began to despise him. Júlio, deeply in love, could not bear to see her smiling at another man she had met and ended up committing suicide. Júlio, then, left his past life connected to Marlene, and their destinies once again crossed in a new incarnation.

In captivity, Marlene felt that someone was trying to help her, yet she looked around and saw no one. Help is not always visible to the eyes of the flesh, and to receive it, we must connect our thoughts with spirituality, saying a heartfelt prayer to calm our hearts and allow the spirits of light to send us good suggestions that can help us solve the most complicated situations.

Ernesto placed his hand on the girl's forehead, sending her energies of peace. Marlene, very depressed, malnourished, and upset, was already giving herself up to death because she did not believe that she would survive that. Little did the girl know that discouragement opens the door to illusion and attracts those who, careless of the good, remain anchored in evil, pretending to cheat life without knowing that they are cheating themselves.

Without knowing that she was not alone, Marlene received from Ernesto good fluids, beneficial energies, healing energies, that fed her weakened spirit, keeping her away from harmful energies.

✶ ✶ ✶

Intuited by Ernesto, Marcos began to follow Júlio's steps everywhere. A victim of his inner unbalance and already full of persecutory ideas, Júlio, even without knowing that he was being watched by Marcos, began to try to hide any connection with the case and began to present suspicious attitudes. He was always nervous, impatient, startled, and even his friends noticed the changes in the boy's countenance. Unfortunate is he who thinks he is able of circumventing the laws of life. God, superior intelligence, primary cause of all things, commands all events always acting for our spiritual growth and development. Sooner or later, the truth appears as a brilliant light to illuminate the darkness of our ignorance.

While still in prison, Marlene, even with all the spiritual help she was receiving from Ernesto, began to get sick and have some spiritual visions. In one of those visions, she had an astral trip in which she visualized a very strong scene with Júlio. The boy was kneeling at her feet, begging for her love.

Believing herself to be at the mercy of her own fate, Marlene surrendered herself more and more to the hardship of the situation in which she found herself. Two young men, under Júlio's command, were watching over her and barely feeding her, and the girl already malnourished body showed signs of fatigue.

Marlene did not know where she was and felt out of sorts, as if she were floating in an abyss, unable to find her way out. The girl's mind could no longer produce logical thoughts, and her arms and legs were numb. She could not even stand up.

Far away from there, but deeply distressed, were Marlene's parents, who, already in disbelief that they would find their daughter alive, were waiting for further news. Poor creatures! They did not understand that the mind is a repetition device that must be commanded by the spirit and that, in a difficult situation, the important thing is to cultivate good thoughts, surrender our afflictions to the spirituality and to ask for a solution to the issues that are beyond our limited knowledge.

And so, the investigations progressed in both cases: Paulo José and Marlene. Several times, Marcos was sure that the cases were connected, but Humberto, the delegate who oversaw the investigation of Paulo José's attack, still had doubts. How would Marcos explain to explain to Humberto that his certainty came from spirituality? Besides, he had no evidence, which made everything even more complex. For the delegate, everything was just supposition.

In the meantime, Julio decided to travel without giving anyone any satisfaction. Before doing so, however, he quickly stopped by the captivity to make the weekly payment to his accomplices.

The news that Julio had traveled had reached Humberto and Marcos through Emilia, who was worried and tried to keep alert of any detail that might help the police to find Marlene.

One day, while talking to Solange, one of Marlene's best friends, Emília heard something that awakened her maternal sixth sense. The girl commented that Marlene had mentioned that she was going through a very difficult situation and did not know how to solve it.

– But what was going on with Marlene, Solange? Tell me! – Distressed, Emilia questioned the girl.

Feeling sorry for her friend's mother's distress, Solange recounted the conversation she had with Marlene. During the conversation, the girl confided that she had done something very unpleasant and that this could have serious consequences, but due to the shame of what had happened, she kept quiet, without revealing the fact to her best friend.

Desperate, Emilia asked Solange if the conversation was recent, and the girl confirmed, but reiterated that she had no idea what Marlene was omitting from her and her family.

– Mrs. Emília, there is someone that Marlene trusted blindly. I know her, because we were together a few times. Who knows, maybe she can help you? It's worth a try.

– Who is this person? Please tell me!

– Her name is Cenira and she's a piano teacher. Her loneliness brought her closer to Marlene, who considers her a very dear friend. We met her at an event at the club. She is not Brazilian.

– Solange, for all that is most sacred to the world, take me to her!

– Of course! Do you want to go now?

Faced with the affirmative answer of the afflicted mother, Solange promptly accompanied Emilia to the piano teacher's house.

Once there, Emilia introduced herself to Cenira and told her about what had happened. Cenira was a very elegant, middle-aged woman whose easy smile captivated everyone. The teacher, aware of what had happened, said she found Marlene's sudden departure strange, because almost every day the girl stopped by her house for coffee and to hear her play the piano. Despite admiring the beautiful melodies Cenira played, Marlene had never been interested in learning to play the instrument.

Hopeful of the possibility of discovering some clue about the whereabouts of her beloved daughter, Emilia explained to Cenira that she was the only chance they had of finding out anything about Marlene, and that João Alberto, the girl's father, was bedridden with a strong depression.

Cenira remained silent and thoughtful.

– I can't talk to you right now. Could you come back later? – said Cenira, laconic.

Despite the frustration on her face, Emilia answered promptly:

– Yes, I can!

***

Time passed slowly until it was time for Emilia to return to Cenira's house. Confident that the teacher would have something important to tell her, the woman rang the house bell expectantly.

After being invited in, Emília sat down on the couch the teacher had indicated in the large and well–decorated living room. The house was well kept, and the details of the decoration attested the good taste of the hostess.

Without further ado, Cenira was direct in asking:

– Do you talk to your daughter?

– Of course. Why?

Cenira was reluctant to tell everything she knew, but analyzing the situation mentally, she concluded that Marlene might be at risk of death and decided to reveal what she knew.

– Mrs. Emília, I am not sure how I will reveal what I know, because it is something very personal. It would be better if Marlene herself told you everything, but given the situation, I will not omit myself – Cenira was categorical: – Your daughter is pregnant!

– Pregnant? What do you mean? – Emília was shocked to hear the revelation.

– Yes! She is pregnant. The last time I saw Marlene, she was very confused because she was not sure who was the child's father. If memory serves me correctly, she told me that she was involved with a boy named Júlio, but she had a fight with him.

Seeing that Emilia paled at every word she heard, Cenira paused briefly, but there was no turning back. That mother needed to know the whole truth, even if it would destroy all her illusions.

Cenira continued the narrative:

– After a fight with Júlio, Marlene mentioned that she went to a party and, although she was not in the habit of drinking, she ended up drinking. Under the effect of alcohol, she ended up giving herself up to another guy. If memory serves me correctly, his name is Paulo José. Shortly after Marlene discovered that she was pregnant, Marlene went to find Júlio to tell him that the child was his. However, to her unhappiness, the boy learned from a friend that Marlene and Paulo José had a relationship. The angry boy told her that the child was not his, and in desperation, Marlene threatened him.

Cenira was silent, because she only knew the story up to that point. After Marlene had told her what happened, she had never seen her again. She was really worried about her friend.

Dismayed by everything she had heard about her daughter, Emilia put her hands on her head, despaired and helplessly, mourned her pain. The poor woman could not understand her daughter's misconduct.

– Where did I go wrong, my God? I have always been a good mother who fulfilled my responsibilities, and I never let Marlene lack anything. My husband is an honorable man and has always taken care of everyone with zeal. How will I tell him that our daughter has tarnished the family name? – she asked herself.

Trapped in her pain, Emília was a slave to appearances, to the dictates of a society incapable of forgiving the outbursts of youth and of understanding the strength of a passion. Marlene, like so many other girls of her age, could not contain her impulses, deluded herself and was being judged by the laws of men. But God, in His infinite wisdom, never accuses His children because He knows that everything in life is learning. There are no mistakes, no judgments; everything is learning.

Cenira tried to calm Emília by asking her to try to understand Marlene, the fact that she was young and had fallen in love.

Emilia thanked Cenira sincerely and said her that she would get help. She explained that, with the information the teacher had revealed to her, she was sure the situation would be resolved in a few days.

On her way home, Emília decided to enter a church to pray and seek spiritual help. Giving free rein to her sadness, the woman prayed fervently. Tears were falling in abundance, and it was at that moment that she heard a soft voice whisper in her ear:

– Her daughter is alive!

Emília was at a loss as to what to do. What would be better? To go back home or to look for delegate Humberto? She decided for the second option. She could not stay still. She had to act and help the police find her daughter.

Shortly afterwards Emília arrived at the police station. After talking to some police officers on duty, she arrived distressed at the delegate's office and knocked lightly on the door.

– Doctor Humberto, excuse me but I need to talk to you. I have some information that may help in the case of my daughter's disappearance.

– Mrs. Emilia, I ask you to sit down and wait a few minutes as I am finishing signing some documents.

– That's fine. I will wait as long as it takes. I am not leaving here until I tell you what I found out.

After about an hour of waiting, the delegate called Emilia, who stumbling over the words, related the whole story told by Cenira.

Humberto remained static, as he had many doubts about what he had heard. The story was very convoluted, with several loose ends, which made the delegate wonder how he would solve this enigma.

Recovering his cool head, Humberto explained to Emília that he would thoroughly investigate everything she had told him and that he would not rest until he found out the truth.

After saying goodbye to Emília, the delegate decided to contact Marcos. In response to a request from Dionísio's and Ignácio, Humberto had agreed to let the boy know about the investigation, even though this was not common protocol in the police. Throughout the meetings with the boy, the delegate nevertheless began to appreciate Marcos' analytical thinking and began to consider the hypotheses he raised. Now, with this new data involving the names of Marlene, Júlio and Paulo José, the investigations of both cases would take new directions.

Later, when Marcos arrived at the police station, Humberto told him what Emília had told him. The boy listened attentively to the delegate's account and showed that he believed the story of Marlene's mother. Without wasting any time, he informed Humberto that he would go in search of corroborating evidence. Life is functional and, whenever it needs it, it finds people willing to help. In this case, Marcos was being instrumental in bringing out the truth and freeing those involved from the debts that hindered their spiritual growth.

After they agreed on some details, and Humberto gave Marcos carte blanche to act according to his impressions, the two men said goodbye.

After leaving the police station, Marcos went in search of Júlio, but he learned that the boy had traveled without telling anyone, and that not even the family knew his destination. Guided by spirituality and with Emilia's testimony, Marcos became more and more convinced that there was a connection between Paulo José's attempt on his life, Marlene's disappearance and Julio's unexpected trip.

***

Out of his mind, Júlio was firm in his resolve not to return home. But what had he planned against Marlene? What orders had he given to the thugs responsible for the girl's captivity?

After days of going from one city to another, disoriented, sleeping in roadside hotels, Júlio arrived in Lorena, in the interior of São Paulo, and settled in a modest hotel located in the city center.

Throughout the trip, Júlio did not feel well, and he was constantly thinking destructive and disturbing thoughts, in which Marlene's image kept popping up. Unvigilant, the boy was tuning into inferior creatures, to evil spirits that wove webs of madness around his disturbed spirit and rejoiced in the pain of others, incapable of making a gesture to help others. Would Júlio come out of this deep state of mental disturbance?

***

It had been more than six days since the last events and no new clues had emerged as to Marlene's whereabouts. With Júlio's unexpected trip, however, attention turned to him, but there was no clue as to where the boy was.

Still in captivity, Marlene was very fragile and felt great pains in her body. She had not had enough to eat for days, but her pregnancy was still going well, because the spirit about to incarnated was being guarded by spirituality. To live a new journey on Earth is something special, and a chance to experience new sensations, to learn about the laws that govern life and to climb steps toward the improvement of the spirit.

Next to the captivity, a hovel that had been the home of Jonas, an old man who died of alcoholism, there was a house in where two women lived: Isaura and her daughter Juana. The woman's husband had died about two years before.

One day, Isaura heard something like a person crying. It sounded like a constant wailing and came from nearby. She, then, told her daughter about her impression, but Joana replied that it could be someone from the family of Jonas, the former resident, and asked her not to get involved in the matter because she had seen two strange people walking around the place. Isaura, however, remained restless, after all, the crying would not go away.

Without listening to Joana's advice, Isaura talked to her friend Aparecida about what had happened. Always together, the two women worked sewing and helped the community by doing charity work.

Aparecida, who was more resourceful, became alert after Isaura's story. Sharpening her ears, she realized that the crying she heard seemed to come from a woman, yet she could only see two men circulating in the house.

– I'm going to the police, Isaura. There is something strange about this story – says Aparecida.

Fearful Isaura warned:

– It can be dangerous, because we don't know what it's about. The best thing is to forget this story. I live alone with Joana in the middle of nowhere. What if they do something against us?

– But do you think I'm not worried about that, Isaura? If these men are involved in something shady, what guarantee do you have that it won't come knocking on your door at some point? Besides, we can't keep quiet about this strange situation. And if the police don't find anything, at least our consciences will be clear. We learn that it's not enough not to do evil! It is also necessary to always do good so that life brings us opportunities for progress – concluded Aparecida.

The woman did not know it, but she was being inspired by good friends of the light, who found in Aparecida a fertile ground for sowing good actions.

For a moment, the woman was still undecided, and a silly idea came to her mind: "What if it was a spirit crying?", but then she shook the thought away with a shrug, something very much her own, which she repeated whenever she wanted to get rid of something. Resolute, Aparecida finally went to the nearest police station.

After a few minutes of waiting, and Dr. Alcides Brandão, the city delegate, received Aparecida and began to listen to the woman's story.

Alcides was an honest man, who honored his more than twenty years of police work. He had never been negligent in his job, and he was there to protect the population and to act within the strictness of the law. After hearing

Aparecida's story, he promptly decided to investigate the suspicions raised by the woman.

Experienced, Alcides knew how to act with prudence in situations of that nature and, with the intention of defusing an eventual criminal action, he sent Samuel and Ricardo, two undercover policemen, to the scene.

After conducting a stakeout in the vicinity of the house, the police officers spotted a light-skinned man in front of the house who appeared to be about thirty years old, sitting on a chair. They carefully continued to watch from a distance to prevent the suspects from escaping.

Samuel and Ricardo returned to the city's police station to report the case to Alcides and come up with a plan of action, which needed to be fast. Although they did not know exactly what they were dealing with, the whole scenario indicated that something was wrong. Was it a simple invasion of private property or was there something behind it? Whose constant crying were Aparecida, and Isaura hearing? And why did those two men seem tense and on alert?

Armed with courage and a sincere desire to help their fellow man, the men, all family fathers, who worked zealously in their profession, moved quickly to the suspected location. They waited for nightfall to fall and, in an orchestrated action, invaded the house and found Marlene lying on a filthy cot, covered with a torn sheet that exuded a foul odor. Frightened, totally dehydrated and malnourished as a result of long days without constant water and food, the girl was promptly rescued and taken to the nearest hospital.

While the girl, in a state of shock, was taken to the hospital in one of the vehicles, the two men guarding Marlene's captivity were taken, already handcuffed, to another vehicle and to the police station. One of the men was called Damião and his criminal record included robbery and swindling; the other, Marcelo, was a frail 20-year-old boy who had no police record.

Although the police had managed to arrest the two men, the case was still far from being clarified. Alcides still did not know who the rescued girl was, why she was being kept in that house and in those conditions and who was behind it all. Seeking answers to his questions, the delegate began a detailed interrogation with the two men who had been arrested.

While they were being interrogated, Damião, the older of the pair, stood firm in the face of the pressure he was under and evasively answered to the delegate's questions. While Marcelo, the other boy, was very afraid, for it was the first time he had been arrested and did not have the wits to withstand the pressure that a police interrogation provoked. Noticing Marcelo's weak point, the delegate was incisive, and after a few hours of psychological pressure, the thief ended up handing over the kidnapping mentor.

– I will say but release me! It was a weakness of mine! I am not a bandit! – said Marcelo with his nerves on edge.

Alcides knew that it would not be possible to release the boy before the trial, but that he could make a deal with him. If he was convicted, his statement would say that he had contributed to the investigations, which would help him to get his sentence reduced. Everything was in the boy's hands, and he had to choose which path to follow. Life always presents us with free will, however, the consequences of our good or bad actions always arrive, no matter how long it takes. Unfortunately, some people still ignore the laws of life and trapped in illusions, have a long way to go to achieve the balance needed to evolve on this earthly journey.

After a few seconds of hesitation, Marcelo finally confessed that Júlio had ordered the kidnapping, thus sealing the boy's fate and that he had to answer to the laws of men for the crime. But what about spirituality? How would it teach him the necessary lessons?

CHAPTER 10

In the hospital, Marlene recovered little by little from the days of terror she had lived in captivity. The girl, still fragile from the recent events, could communicate, although she was visibly traumatized. Malnourished and a little dehydrated, Marlene questioned all the time if the child she was carrying in her womb was all right.

Marlene arrived at the hospital immersed in a deep state of mental confusion due to days of deprivation of water and enough food to sustain her life. She arrived at the health unit with disconnected thoughts, slurred speech and glassy eyes, searching for answers to everything she had been through and especially for familiar faces.

Alcides, upon learning of the girl's condition, decided to wait a few days before trying to question her. In the end, no one knew who Marlene was, where she came from or if she had any relatives. The only information the delegate had at this point was the name of the name of the person who ordered the crime and that the man lived in Rio de Janeiro.

When Marlene finally showed considerable improvement, that is, when her thoughts and speech became connected again, Alcides was able to question her and discovered that the girl came from a wealthy family in Rio de Janeiro. Having Marlene's family's phone number and address, the delegate was able to contact the girl's parents and inform them of their daughter's whereabouts.

Still in disbelief, João Alberto and Emília received a telegram from Alcides and then a phone call from the delegate who told them objectively what had happened and gave the address of the hospital where the girl was hospitalized. With this information, the couple called the delegate Humberto and informed him that Marlene had been found.

– Yes, Dr. Humberto. Marlene has been found. My daughter was being kept in a house in the middle of nowhere! The city delegate, Dr. Alcides, said they found her thanks to a tip. They went to check the place believing it was a case of trespassing and found her in a deplorable state. My daughter...

Still very nervous, João Alberto narrated the latest events to Humberto, because he was the delegate officially in charge of the case of Marlene's disappearance.

– Mr. João, I will be on my way there and I'll meet you at the hospital. As soon as I settle a few loose ends here, I will hit the road.

– We are leaving the house in a little while. I just want to see my daughter.

✱ ✱ ✱

Hours later, João Alberto and Emília arrived at the hospital where Marlene was hospitalized. Emotional and still in disbelief that she had been found alive, the girl's parents let their tears flow freely.

Emília, the girl's mother, was already aware of everything, but she could not hide how shocked she was by the events and her daughter's pregnancy. Fragile, many people create models of behavior that are considered perfect and become frustrated when others do not fit into these standards. Emília was suffering with the crumbling of her illusions, without accepting that she was just being visited by the truth, which is liberating.

Humberto, the delegate in charge of the case, arrived at the hospital a short time later, but decided to ask the girl a few questions, as he realized that Marlene was still very shaken psychologically. He preferred to focus his questions on Alcides, so he soon went to the police station of the small town, where he confirmed the name of the person responsible for the crime: Júlio. The same Júlio that Marcos pointed out as a strong suspect.

✱ ✱ ✱

Still in the city of Lorena, Júlio kept away from everyone. Every day the boy became more taciturn and irascible, searching for a culprit for his afflictions.

Júlio's preventive custody had already been issued by a court, which had happened to the testimony of Marcelo, one of the men who held Marlene captive under orders from the boy, and the testimony of the girl who, even though still very traumatized, was able to report her capture and confirm her involvement in love with Júlio.

In tune with inferior spirits, who delighted in leading their fellow men to physical and moral decadence, Julio sought refuge in drink. The boy, trapped in the mental weaknesses that only an unbalanced soul is capable of feeling, was completely out of his mind.

Tormented by having kidnapped Marlene and, consequently, by having committed a crime, Júlio knew that the path he had chosen had no turning back and that he would have to pay for his crime. The certainty that he had made a wrong move would made him desperate and run away. Without knowing that his accomplices had been arrested and that Marlene had been released from captivity, Júlio, locked in a hotel, was still thinking about what he would do with his ex–girlfriend and how he would escape from prison. The last time he had been with the goons, he had paid them a month's service in advance and left money for Marlene's food expenses, but soon that money would run out and he would have to decide what to do. He would need to go back, but he feared being arrested. He felt trapped by his wrong choices.

One afternoon, already tired of the confinement in the hotel and completely drunk, he decided to drive off in his car. Bewildered, Júlio began to be delirious and to hear voices. In his profound state of mental disturbance, he could not understand that it was time to accept the inevitable and recognize that crying, lamenting and rebelling were useless attitudes. The boy did not know that life always goes on, that the challenges it brings are measured according to our need to learn, and that each one of them only arises when we already have the knowledge to overcome them. Life does not play to lose and only bets on winning. Our spirit has everything we need to carry on our growth process, whether we are incarnated or disincarnated.

Júlio was sweating, and his hands were shaking as he tried, unsuccessfully, to keep the car moving in a straight line through the streets. Zigzagging, he managed to get out of Lorena and onto the road, where he could gain more speed.

The more anguish assaulted his chest, the more Júlio dug his foot into the accelerator of the car, which was already shaking from the high speed. Suddenly, without being able to see the road clearly, because the tears had already overcome his eyes, Julio lost control of the car, overturning three times in a row and leaving a trail of destruction on the asphalt.

A man on the road witnessed the accident and went to Lorena to get help. As soon as he was able to report what had incident to a police station, an ambulance was sent to the scene, but there was no time to save Julio's life. He was badly injured and still trapped in the wreckage; the boy died.

As he carried in his pocket a wallet with his documents and a phonebook, Julio's body was identified, and the police tried to find someone in his contacts list that belonged to the boy's family. When they finally managed to talk to Júlio's parents, already very upset about the disappearance of their son and the accusation that he had ordered the kidnapping of Marlene, the news of the boy's death hit them like a bomb, devastating them.

A lot of suffering took over everyone who lived with that suffering spirit, tormented by illusions created by an idle mind that did not seek personal fulfillment and assistance to others through work. Besides the shock of receiving the police at home with a preventive arrest warrant for Júlio, the boy's parents were now faced with the news of the boy's death. Fortunately, however, everything is right in life, and what seems like the end is only a pause for our recovery, certain that we will have other opportunities for our development.

After the court was informed of Julio's death, the investigation proceeded normally, obeying the legal procedures. Sometime later, Damião and Marcelo were indicted, tried and convicted for the crime of kidnapping and private captivity.

* * *

Back home, Marlene, on medical advice, continued to rest, since her pregnancy was at risk due to so many misfortunes. The girl had not yet fully recovered from the trauma and her condition worsened after she found out who had ordered the kidnapping. She could not believe that Julio was capable of such a vile act. And if the police had not rescued her, what would have been her fate? Would she still be alive? What had he planned against her? Faced with so many questions, Marlene, unknowingly connected to inferior energies, creating a negative egregore around her, which attracted ignorant spirits indifferent to compassion and love for others.

Between the seventh and eighth month of pregnancy, Marlene began to have severe pains in her belly, that soon turned out to be the messenger of premature birth. The girl gave birth to a very fragile and small baby girl. Soon after birth, the baby needed to be assisted by doctors because she was born with very weak lungs. The baby needed to be promptly referred to the Neonatal ICU, where she was under intensive medical care, aiming at her development.

The spirit's reincarnation is often a delicate moment because he will have to prepare himself emotionally, according to the problems he still has and the progress he wishes to achieve. In this process, some fear the return, because they know that they will have to forget the past, face the unknown, test their knowledge, take responsibilities for choosing their own path; but all of them, without exception, are supported by spirits of light, who watch over them and help them with good advice. All that is needed is to trust in life and embrace with faith the good opportunities.

And so, the lives of our characters followed the natural course of events. Some, by choosing tortuous paths, made pain their companion on the journey; but in their own time and in their own way, they would learn the precious lessons of life, that would lead them to happiness.

✳ ✳ ✳

After the period of upheaval so common to recently disincarnated spirits, Júlio, not accepting death, began to wander desperately in search of Marlene. The boy's spirit, weak and badly injured from the accident, felt vividly the injuries occurred in the flesh body, because he was still attached to the impressions of the material world.

The spirituality, however, never abandons the creatures that need help to understand their current state and move on, because becoming a better human being is the primordial task of all spirits. For this we incarnate as many times as necessary to evolve morally, following the lessons that Christ left us.

In order to help him, Júlio was visited by his grandmother, who tried to rescue him and take him to a spiritual colony, where he would receive help and begin his recovery. The boy did not accept the help of the kindly lady and said he did not want to move on until he freed Marlene from captivity, not knowing that the girl had already been rescued. Tired, hurt, and trapped by mental disturbances, Júlio, not knowing the mechanisms that make it possible for us to move through the astral spheres, tried, in vain, to find the place where he had kept Marlene.

Lost, Júlio began to ally himself with mocking spirits, believing that with them he would find a way, and in this disturbance, he wandered through lower regions, where a dense and fetid fog caused the spirits still attached to the impressions of the physical body to suffocate. The boy felt cold, hungry, tired, and only a vague idea of his present condition sometimes came to his mind.

Suddenly, Júlio remembered his childhood, of the joy he shared with his friends in the always lively children's games. Among so many friendly faces, one of them appeared strongly in the boy's memory. It was as if that person was there, at that moment, within reach of his hands. Enveloped by that impression, Julio felt as if he were quickly floating away, as if he were crossing distances, exploring regions, and an intense heat took over his spirit. The next thing he knew, he found himself in the house of Francisco, his best childhood friend, who had shown a marked mediumship from early age.

Francisco's parents did not take the boy's mediumship seriously and believed that their son talked to imaginary friends. Francisco, on the other hand, felt the presence of his deceased grandparents and connected without fear with the invisible world.

Time went by and Francisco, even though he believed in interchange with the spirituality, remained unvigilant, resistant to study and spiritual education. The boy had no bad character but living like this he attracted both good and bad spirits.

As soon as he heard of Julio's death, Francisco began to pray to God that his friend would be supported wherever he was. On that particular day, he felt a strong presence of Julio, who, furious, could not understand why Francisco ignored him and made a mockery of his presence.

– Francisco, can't you see me here? Hey! Are you deaf?!

From then on, Francisco became a victim of Júlio's unbalance, who, in order to attract the boy's attention, turned the lights on and off and moved objects around, with the intention of being noticed without realizing that he was in another dimension, on another plane, and that he had no right to act arbitrarily against his incarnate brothers.

One rainy night, Francisco lay down and sleep came soon. The boy, who worked with his father, was tired because the day had been exhausting. In the middle of the night, he was awakened by Júlio's voice that called clearly for him. It was a cry for help. He was sure of it.

Startled and still sleepy, Francisco sat up and began to pray for Júlio, feeling goose bumps all over his body. With a racing heart he heard lamentations and a cry of pain.

Armed with courage, Francisco asked:

– Júlio, is that you there?

At that moment, the water jug that was next to Francisco's bed was thrown to the floor.

Moved by a sincere desire to help his friend, Francisco continued to pray until everything calmed down, and finally he could go back to sleep.

The next day, already recovered, Francisco got up thinking about everything that had happened last night. The boy wondered aloud:

– My God, what is happening? How can I help my friend? Who will believe what has happened? They will think I'm crazy for seeing a dead person!

Good friends of light heard Francisco's questions and, recognizing the true feeling of brotherly love that he emanated, they went to help him in support his friend.

Filled with deleterious energies that brutalized his spirit, Júlio, however, could not bear the good energies of those spirits of light and, inconsequently, fled the place.

Júlio wandered for many hours thinking about everything that had happened. Francisco's words still reverberated in his mind. So, it was true. He really was dead. Yes, he had already suspected some of the perceptions he had experienced but to hear from his childhood friend about his new condition was disturbing. The memories of past actions came overwhelmingly to his mind. What had he done with his life? And how would he deal with the people he had hurt? How would he move on if he was dead? What would come next?

Júlio's conscience charged him the just price for his actions, because illusions bring pain, only truth teaches and sets free. We do not always accept change because we are used to seeing only what is favorable to us, we believe that everything in our life must follow our will; however, the need for progress moves things around and traces more lucid and profitable paths.

Nothing remains static and thoughts are no different. Faced with the truth, Júlio wanted to free himself from his anguish and so the despair of finding Marlene and Paulo José became lacerating to him.

Despite his sincere willingness to pay his past debts, Julio remained disturbed, feeling a kind of exhaustion caused by the unbalanced energies. In search of relief for the affliction that afflicted him, he left without direction and, without realizing it, became easy prey for the deleterious fluids that came from the drunks and chemical addicts of that region. And unfortunately, vibrating in that tune, he distanced himself from Francisco, the only path to the realization of his projects.

CHAPTER 11

Time passed quickly. The colorful flowers adorned the garden of Marlene's house. It was late afternoon, and a soft breeze was blowing. The peace that exhaled from the outside contrasted with the storm of feelings that the residents of the house were facing.

Marlene was still recovering from the trauma of the kidnapping, the days of terror in captivity and the birth of her daughter Maria Helena, a beautiful, blue-eyed, smiling little girl.

Little by little, the girl's family also tried to overcome the latest events, but they often faltered. João Alberto and Emília, slaves of society's dictates, mulled over the past and regretted everything that had happened to their daughter.

– My daughter, I know that your father and I are often angry about what happened but understand... we are imperfect. I see in your eyes that you are also ashamed of what happened; but let's move on. We cannot forget that, during this tragedy, God gave us an angel.

– Mom, sometimes it seems that I am still falling off a cliff and, at other times, I feel that little by little, my joy for living is returning to my heart.

– Marlene, our family is all about me, you, your father and our angel Maria Helena. We must fight. I know it is difficult to deal with the criticism from society and I confess that it is not rare that I falter, but I have chosen to think of you both, of our family that is what really matters. Come on, daughter! We must overcome everything that has happened.

What the two women did not know was that, in parallel to all the situations that had befallen the family, João Alberto was still facing problems in the company. He had, however, decided to keep what was happening from them, so as not to worry them.

It all started when Marlene disappeared from home. Distressed not to hear from his daughter, João Alberto neglected the company's administration and ended up delegating decisions to incompetent and unscrupulous employees, who gradually led the company to bankruptcy.

Distressed, the head of the family kept quiet, trying to solve the adversities. To try to save the company from bankruptcy, João Alberto sold part of the company's shares to a businessman in the industry, Carlos, who, with his son Raul, would be the new partner. Thus, João Alberto decided to step away from the management.

Very radical and mercenary, Carlos was preparing to take the company from João Alberto's hands and planned to buy the shares of a minority partner, to hold the majority of the company's shares.

Raul, however, was a good boy and had a fair and unblemished character and opposed his father's plans, arguing that João Alberto deserved more respect for the difficult time he was going through.

And so, the days went by.

Without realizing it, João Alberto was stricken with a deep depression. The once active and always cheerful businessman gradually lost the will to work, to talk to his daughter and wife and to live. He even left his granddaughter, who was the light of his life, aside.

Concerned with the father's growing apathy, Marlene decided to tell her mother about her impressions and that she had noticed a strong odor of drink coming from the father.

– Marlene, my daughter, your father was never a drinking man. You must be mistaken.

– Mom, I smelled it more than once. Let's pay attention.

– I can't believe that! – Emília answered dryly, with the purpose of ending that unpleasant subject.

Besides constantly indulging in drink, João Alberto was no longer eating properly. It seemed that this hard-working man, full of life, was slowly dying.

Even though she believed that Marlene was mistaken about her father, Emília went to João Alberto to make sure that everything was right. She was not a bad wife, however, unable to deal with situations that were beyond her control, she preferred to lock herself up in her world of appearances, often ignoring the hardships of her own family. This was the case with Marlene's pregnancy and now with her husband's illness.

***

Time ran on unabated and indifferent to the afflictions of Marlene's family.

Worried about João Alberto's health, Raul decided to look for Emília and tell her everything that was going on. Resolute, the young man went to the partner's house and was received by the matriarch of the Fiorucci family, who did not understand the reason for that visit.

In a few words, Raul told Emília about João Alberto's constant absence from the company.

The two were talking so much in the living room that they did not notice Marlene's arrival in the room. The girl heard the boy's last words and, astonished, asked:

– Raul, my father always took care of the company with great zeal. What is going on?

– I can't explain the reason, but he hardly stays there and doesn't manage anything else. He seems disgusted with life.

Marlene then lowered her head and began to cry, blaming herself for everything. In her heart, the girl believed that the fact that she had gotten pregnant and was raising Maria Helena without a father was the reason for João Alberto's grief. Seeing her daughter weakened, Emília hugged Marlene and said:

– Calm down, daughter. We'll work it all out!

João Alberto did not know about Raul's visit, as Emília had asked him not to tell anyone.

Emília began to observe her husband better and noticed that he often smelled of drink. The woman, however, decided to keep silent.

One day, Emilia went to accompany Marlene to the doctor and, when the mother and daughter returned home, they found João Alberto lying on the couch in the living room, completely drunk. Emília even tried to talk to her husband, but as he could not utter a word, Marlene said:

– Mom, there is no point in talking now. Dad is in no condition to talk now.

– Yes... you are right, my daughter.

João Alberto woke up that late at night vomiting heavily. Embarrassed, he could not even look at his wife, because she had always seen him as a very strong man.

The next day, Marlene asked Emília to leave her alone with her father. Determined to put an end to the situation, the girl went to her father:

– Dad, can we talk a little?

– Yes, daughter.

– What's going on with you?

– Nothing, my daughter. I'm tired and I overdid it a little. I needed to relax and resorted to drinking.

– Father, for God's sake, can you understand that you'll only hurt yourself with that? I know you've been abandoning everything, and I feel guilty for this situation.

– Marlene, if there is a guilty party, it is me, daughter. Nothing that is happening has anything to do with you. I failed!

– Dad, let's work it out! I want to be by your side! I hope you trust me. I know I made a mistake, but my feet are on the ground, and I will help you.

João Alberto did not want to accept the daughter's help, because he believed that it was the man's responsibility to support the family. Moreover, how could he leave his prejudice aside and receive help from a woman? Unfortunately, he placed too great burden on himself and was unable to understand that men and women are equally competent and capable of running a business. Finally, overcome with fatigue, he replied:

– It's ok, daughter.

João Alberto then revealed to Marlene that he often felt he was not alone and thought a lot about his father, Moisés, who had lost everything to drinking and gambling. Desperate, the man confided to his daughter that he was also gambling and drinking too much and that he had walked away from the company.

Marlene's father was relieved after talking to the daughter, because he had been keeping all those problems for a long time, which caused him deep discomfort. That moment was one of unit and great complicity between them. Father and daughter embraced and there, without words, they sealed a loyalty pact: they would always count on each other, regardless of the situation.

＊＊

The next day Marlene woke up and went to find her father. Resolute, she had decided. The girl asked João Alberto for permission to help him manage the company. Her father, despite the conversation they had the night before, was still reluctant, but eventually agreed to let Marlene work in the company.

Marlene asked Emilia to take care of Maria Helena so she could work.

– Marlene, my daughter, I am very happy! Don't worry! I will be very happy to take care of my granddaughter.

– Mom, don't worry. I'll take care of dad and the company. Everything will be fine. He needs my help.

The girl decided, for the time being, not to tell Emília that João Alberto, besides having developed an addiction to alcohol, was addicted to gambling. She would wait a little longer. She was sure that the solution would come soon, without having to worry her mother even more.

And so, Marlene started working for the company. Inspired by friends of light, the girl prayed hard that everything would turn out well.

At first, Carlos did not like Marlene's presence in the company, but the girl was very friendly and gradually won over even the most difficult people. João Alberto's partner, who used to be grumpy and bad-tempered, softened his heart and accepted the girl willingly.

As time went by, Raul and Marlene began to get along very well together. In tune, the two young people brought good ideas to the business and happily accompanied the company's growth.

Almost a year had passed since the last events and Marlene continued to help her father in the administration of the company. In parallel, João Alberto decided to seek specialized treatment to cure his addiction to drinking and gambling.

Marlene became a close friend of Raul's, who had confided in her that he was homosexual and had been in a stable relationship with Roberto for more than three years. The two loved each other very much and planned to live in Portugal. Raul's parents never suspected anything, and Marlene was the only one who knew everything.

– Raul, I would like you to baptize my daughter.

– Marlene, I don't believe it! Of course, I accept the invitation! What happiness! I love Maria Helena!

– That's wonderful! The godparents will be you and my cousin Judith.

The girl was growing up and becoming more beautiful every day. Júlio, in spirit, visited her many times to visit the daughter and Marlene could feel his presence. However, the girl had not told Maria Helena about her father, because the girl was still too young.

CHAPTER 12

One night, Francisco arrived home very tired. The day had been exhausting and he just wanted to take a shower and go straight to sleep, because he had already had a quick meal outside.

The boy was already in bed when a restlessness began to take over him. Rolling from side to side in bed, Francisco could not get to sleep.

Suddenly, Francisco felt a strong smell of booze in his room, but he thought it was only an impression. Little did the boy know that it was Júlio who had arrived there accompanied by Eduardo, a spirit who had died of an overdose at the age of 22.

When Eduardo was nine years old, he was involved in an accident, in which he lost his father and an aunt, Sara. His mother and brother survived, but since then, he has become rebellious. At the age of 16, Eduardo was already on the road to drugs and at the age of 22, he overdosed and died alone in his room.

After some time, Eduardo regretted that he had caused his own death, but although he was aware that he had disincarnated, he did not accept his new condition and still wandered around. On one of these walks, Eduardo found

Júlio and, after hearing the story of his new friend, decided to help him ask Marlene and Paulo José for forgiveness.

✷ ✷ ✷

Marlene was in a good moment of her life, with a very calm mind and wanting to make changes.

Maria Helena had been baptized by Raul and Judite, the godparents chosen by the girl.

– You know, Marlene – Raul said –, I would really like to start my own business and follow another profession. Roberto has been talking to me about living in Portugal and I have been thinking about this possibility, but I don't know how the company will be if I leave and if you leave. How will our parents be like?

– Raul, we must go in search of our desires and our joys. We cannot follow a path that no longer fulfills us or because of someone else. We all have the right to happiness, and each of us is responsible for our personal fulfillment. Longing is natural, but it should not be a reason for sadness.

– You are right, but deep down I still feel insecure, because my father is getting older, and I might have to take over the company for good. My brother Rogério doesn't want to work with us, and his wife doesn't like our family very much.

– Look, Raul, in due time everything will work out. Trust me! I'm sure that you and Roberto will manage to set up a bakery in Portugal.

– Wow, Marlene, if this happened, my dream would come true. I'd love to be like you! Strong, optimistic!

– Rest assured. Maria Helena and I will always visit you.

Raul's eyes filled with tears, because he considered Heleninha – as he called his goddaughter – a daughter.

✳ ✳ ✳

Each day, Maria Helena became more and more attached to her grandmother Emília. The little girl was already walking and babbling a few words.

With the company financially balanced, Marlene wanted to start her own business but did not yet have in mind in which field she would like to operate. The girl had planned to talk to her father about it but decided to wait a little longer to mature the idea. She thought of many things, but nothing was concrete. The only thing she wanted was to take control of her life and raise Maria Helena.

João Alberto, in turn, was very dependent on his daughter. Marlene had become his father's right–hand man in the company, which made her very worried, because she felt torn between continuing to work with him and facing the independence of opening her own business.

One day, while talking to Raul, Marlene was able to conclude:

– I can find someone else to be my father's right–hand man! – Marlene said.

– Of course, but that's not an easy task Marlene, because your father is not an easy person to deal with and he has his ways. You, being his daughter, are already used to Mr. João and you understand him well. I have my dreams, but Roberto and I can wait a little longer to make them come true. If you need, I can stay a little longer in the company. The important thing is that you can solve your life.

– Oh, Raul, you are a brother to me! I can't thank you enough for everything you have done for us. Thanks to you, the company did not go bankrupt. You know that I will be eternally grateful to you, don't you?

– Dear, me who is grateful to you for letting me be part of your and Heleninha's life. I admire you very much for all the strength you have. I admire you very much for all the strength you have. How many challenges have you faced, huh? You faced the horror of a kidnapping, the responsibility of raising a daughter alone in our society and, after all that you still had to help your father to rebuild the company where the family's livelihood comes from!

Raul embraced Marlene lovingly, like a brother who takes sister in his arms, and with watery eyes, the girl let loose the tears that insisted on flowing. They were, however, tears of uncontained happiness, of knowing that, despite all the difficulties, life, with its grandiose strength, always finds ways to flourish.

CHAPTER 13

Life is like a jigsaw puzzle. Many times, nothing seems to make sense until someone picks up the loose pieces and puts them in their proper place. God always plays this role and, little by little, with His loving fatherly hand, He helps the children to put together that big and complex puzzle that is life, making everything fit together and take shape. And, when we least expect it, the path to follow is revealed to us, all we must do is follow, with faith and hope, the designs from on high.

Emília received a visit from Juliana, her brother Osmar's daughter. The girl was about to get married and went to deliver the invitation to her aunt and other relatives.

– Juliana, how happy I am! Ah, my niece! Of course, we will! Marlene will be very happy with this news.

– Aunt, how are Marlene and Maria Helena? I would love to see them.

– Marlene went to take Maria Helena to the doctor, but everything is fine. It's just a routine appointment.

– Auntie, I know I will ask you an indiscreet question, so you don't need to answer if you don't feel comfortable. But, what about Maria Helena's father? Didn't he take care over the little girl?

– Juliana, my dear, the boy died in an accident.

– Wow, Aunt! I didn't know. How sad! My father didn't say anything.

– My niece, we try not to talk too much about it, because it's a sad and delicate situation. I have asked your father to keep a low profile.

– It's okay, Auntie, don't worry. I also know how to be discreet.

Juliana was a very good girl, with no malice in her heart. Although she had no direct contact with Marlene, she sincerely loved her cousin and hopped for her happiness.

✶ ✶ ✶

Emília was thrilled with her niece's wedding, an event that definitely brought out her vain, feminine side. The Fiorucci matriarch glimpsed several dress models for the occasion and, euphorically arranged with Marlene to go out and buy cuts of fabric so that the tailor could make a beautiful outfit for each of them.

The two women were scheduled to go shopping at the weekend and went downtown to look for fabrics. They entered a store that was well known for selling fine fabrics, that yielded dresses with a great fit.

Mother and daughter were so busy with the task that their attention was only aroused when they heard someone calling for Marlene. Surprised, the girl looked away, but did not recognize anyone.

– Hi Marlene, don't you recognize me? It's me, Lourdes Moreira. Do you remember me?

Lourdes was a childhood friend of Marlene. Both had studied at the same school and were very close when they were young.

– Wow, Lourdes! Is that you! Of course, I remember! Sorry I didn't recognize you, but you look so different! What are you doing here?

– We came to choose some fabrics! – the girl answered cheerfully.

The two girls talked for a while and arranged to have coffee a few days.

On the way home, Emília was also very happy that her daughter had found an old friend again.

Lourdes, in turn, was also happy with this reunion. She could not even imagine what had happened to her friend during the time they had been apart.

***

The week went by quickly, and Thursday arrived. Lourdes and Marlene had arranged to meet at a charming confectioner in an elegant part of town and were very anxious to catch up.

Lourdes told Marlene that she had arrived from Italy about a month ago. The girl had taken a course in dressmaking and kindly offered to make Marlene and Emília's dresses for the wedding.

– Wow, Lourdes, I can't believe you're a stylist! What a joy! Of course, Mom and I will accept that you make our dresses, but you will have to charge for the service.

– Never, Marlene! It's a gift from me to you.

– Thank you very much. I'm sure they'll be beautiful. You always had good taste. But tell me! How are your parents and your brother?

– Ah, my friend, it's a long story... My father got involved with a friend's wife, got her pregnant and left us. It was a scandal! My mother almost went mad, and I had to grow up before my time, because she went into a deep depression. Those were very hard times. I had to take care of my brother Maurício alone. After six years of my parents' separation, my mother got lung cancer and left. Only my brother and I are left. My father rarely came to visit us. He had a daughter, Beatriz, and for some reason that I don't understand to this day, he seems to have forgotten about the children of the first marriage. I guess he decided to concentrate on his new family. My brother and I became even closer, and he managed to get a degree in engineering. Maurício got married and had a beautiful son. Finally, I decided to go to Italy to improve my profession because I want to open a studio.

– Wow Lourdes... I can't imagine how many difficulties you have been through, my friend. I am so sorry about your mother. I remember the times I used to go to your house, and she always welcomed me with warmth. I wish I could have been there for you to help you face with this situation. Marlene was sincerely shaken by all that Lourdes had faced.

The girls continued to exchange confidences. There were so many things they wanted to share. To relax a little, Marlene decided to ask:

– Lourdes, I would like to know more about your professional plans. Do you already have a project for this studio?

– Well, I've been looking for a place where I can open my business. I passed in front of a commercial spot on a very busy street. A lot of stores are opening there.

Marlene thought for a while and decided to take a chance:

– And what do you think about having a partner? I am looking to open a business of my own, but I don't know yet in which area. Since I've been running my father's company, I think I'm very good at managing!

– We will mature this idea. It would be great to have you as a partner. We can try. Let's schedule a coffee meeting next Saturday to talk about it?

– Of course! Deal then!

The friends talked a little bit more. They were happy and full of plans.

***

When Marlene got home, she was euphoric. Without wasting any time, she wanted to tell her mother all the news about her meeting with Lourdes.

– Mom, you won't believe what I have to tell you.

– What is it, daughter?

– Lourdes will make our dresses for Ju's wedding party! She graduated in fashion; she is a stylist and went to Italy to specialize. There she learned a lot about fashion! – Marlene was so excited that she didn't even wait for her mother to answer. Now, Mom, the best part! We're thinking of opening a studio together!

– Daughter, what a good thing. But what about your father?

– Calm down, Mom, I will still talk to Dad. Raul is taking care of everything, and Dad considers him like a son. Everything will be fine!

– Yes, daughter, I believe and trust Raul very much. I am very happy to see that life has brought you together again. I remember very well when you were kids, and you did everything together. How I miss those days!

Mother and daughter continued to weave projects for the future. Peace had finally returned to that home. The challenges were faced with determination by the family that continued firmly on the path of progress.

***

A few days later, Maria Helena woke up with a fever. Emília, faced with the situation, decided to tell Marlene, who had already left for work.

– Mom, what happened to Maria Helena?

– She woke up burning up with fever, daughter. We must take her to Dr. Elza.

The girl left the company in a hurry and returned home to find her mother. Together, they went to the pediatrician's office who had been following Maria Helena's development since the first days of her life.

During the appointment with Dr. Elza, Maria Helena began to have a vomiting crisis, and the pediatrician, evaluating some of the patient's symptoms, asked Marlene and Emília to take the girl to the hospital to be submitted to some tests. The doctor suspected that Maria Helena had meningitis.

Emília despaired. The grandmother could hardly speak, so distressed was she by her granddaughter's clinical condition. Marlene, more practical, took charge of the situation and hushed to the hospital indicated by the doctor.

Those minutes were too harrowing for the two women. What would happen to Maria Helena? Inside a cab, mother and daughter kept quiet, praying.

When they finally arrived at the hospital, Maria Helena was seen by Dr. Adilson, an excellent doctor with a career spanning thirty years. Experienced, the pediatrician immediately realized that the case was serious and, without wasting any time, referred the child for tests.

The situation was delicate. After the results, the suspicions were confirmed: Maria Helena had contracted meningitis, and the case of the little girl was serious. They quickly put the patient in a room, in isolation, where she could not have contact with her family. Only the team of doctors and nurses would have access to her.

Emília began to cry because she had lost a sister to meningitis when she was only eight years old. The woman's despair was so great that the doctors had to medicate her.

Marlene did not know what to do. When she finally calmed down a little, she warned João Alberto and Raul about the girl's serious health condition. Worried, the two men went to the hospital and, together, they faced hours of pain and anguish. In these moments of distress, connecting with spirituality is the best solution. By putting into God's hands, we humbly affirm that we believe in His power and count on His compassion to give us the comfort we need.

Inspired by the friends of light, Raul took Emília to the hospital chapel so she could calm down and, together, they prayed for Maria Helena's recovery.

The boy was very loving and sincerely sympathized with the family's pain. Through prayer, Emília felt that the faith in her heart grow stronger and gradually she was overcome with a great inner peace.

In the days that followed, the family became more confident as Maria Helena began to respond to the medications and was moved to the room, which indicated that the little girl was already out of danger.

In times of distress, divine providence always sends us good friends to support us. They are ordinary people but endowed with a great desire to help others by sharing their good feelings with those in need.

This is how Mercedes, a very spiritual family friend, came along and offered to accompany Marlene to the hospital.

There, the two women began a moving prayer. At that moment, Mercedes felt a shiver run through her body. It was Júlio approaching. Uncomfortable with this sensation, the woman asked him to move away.

Mercedes, not knowing who it was, commented to Marlene about the presence of a man there.

– Mrs. Mercedes, this man might be Maria Helena's father, Júlio, who died in an accident. He was the one who had me kidnapped. He never admitted that I was pregnant.

– Marlene, he is very disturbed. This boy needs help.

– But, Mrs. Mercedes, what can I do for him?

– Look my daughter, this is harmful to you and your daughter. He can't be wandering around. I know that maybe what I say is against your principles, but I need to enlighten you about the truths of the spiritual life. You know that I am part of a group that holds sessions of desobsession. I don't know how to tell you, but it would be very good if you went there so that we could help this boy to free himself.

– Mrs. Mercedes, I would even like to go there with you, because I often feel Júlio's presence, but I am very afraid.

– Marlene, you have no reason to fear. We are just a group of people who dedicate ourselves to matters of spirituality. The center has a leader, Mr. Gabriel, who is already very old and knowledgeable, and a mentor who accompanies the house, brother Lázaro, who disincarnated at 32 years old and was a lawyer in his last incarnation. He passed away from cancer of the intestine. He was a very enlightened spirit in his missions. Dr. Lázaro, as we call him, always comes with his team of workers to accompany our work.

– Can I think a little bit before I decide to go? – Marlene asked.

– Of course. Make yourself at home. I don't want you to feel obligated to come to the meeting. You need to be open-hearted.

✱✱✱

Later, when she arrived home, Marlene commented to her mother about the conversation she had had with Mercedes. Emília didn't even wait for her daughter to finish speaking and promptly said that she would go there, regardless of Marlene's wishes. She wanted to help Júlio free himself and move on.

– Let's go, my daughter! Mercedes is a very good, charitable lady who helps a lot of people!

– Mom, I'm afraid!

– Face this fear, for it will help you and Maria Helena, my daughter. I will accompany you. If you need to, we can talk to Raul. I'm sure he won't refuse to accompany us.

Later, convinced by her mother, Marlene called Mercedes, and, during the conversation, she learned that the next session at the center would take place the following Tuesday.

Under the care of Marlene and her grandmother, Maria Helena improved visibly. The child was already at home, and her flushed face showed that the worst was over.

Even though she was reluctant to leave her daughter under the responsibility of the maid, Marlene decided to go to the session accompanied by Emília and Raul, who, as soon as he learned of the girl's decision to seek help at the center, offered to accompany her.

When they arrived at the simple but neat house, they were warmly received by Mercedes, who was very happy to see them. In her heart, the woman was sure that Marlene had made the right decision, since she would receive help in Júlio's case.

The session started, and Marlene began to tremble. Júlio, however, did not speak up. To everyone's surprise, Raul's aunt, who had committed suicide at the age of 19, appeared with a message for the boy. The woman asked him to take his mother there. It was a great emotion, as Raul's family did not know why the young woman had taken her own life. In the message that had been psychographed by a medium from the house, it said:

"It was a weakness to attempt against my life. Since I was ten years old, I felt very depressed, but I could not identify where that deep sadness came from. When I passed away, I suffered a lot until I could count on the help of my great-grandmother. Only a long time later, I realized that I had reincarnated to overcome the pain of depression. I came to overcome, but I weakened again. Send my love to all my sisters. I went to visit Amélia, who is sick, but she will get better. I ask you to forgive me. A big hug for all of you."

Raul was thrilled to hear his aunt's psychographed words, and later, when he delivered the message to his mother, she cried a lot and told her son that she would also like to go to the sessions.

Marlene was disappointed that Júlio did not show up. Even though she had been told by Mercedes that there was a possibility that the boy would not show up, the girl did not understand the reason for this, since he had shown willingness to communicate: "Why, then, did he not take the opportunity?", she asked herself.

Raul, in turn, could not wait to attend another session at the center and commented on what had happened with Roberto, who also expressed a desire to see the place.

The other day, while they were talking in the company, Marlene started laughing after Raul commented that he and Roberto were looking forward to another session.

– Wow, Raul, I don't believe it! Soon even Dad will want to go to the sessions! – the girl laughed.

CHAPTER 14

A few days later, Marlene and Lourdes met again to discuss business. The two friends finally decided that they would set up the atelier together. From that day on, they would officially become partners.

– Marlene, I suggest that we visit today that commercial site I that I mentioned. If you like the place, we'll close a deal! I believe this is the first step towards open our atelier. We also need to buy two more sewing machines. I already have many dresses designed for us to start working on, because I brought many sketches from Italy.

– That's great, Lourdes! Let's visit that place as soon as possible.

– I have already spoken with the owner. He only required a guarantor and an advance deposit – Lourdes explained.

– There is no problem about them. My father can be our guarantor. That's settled!

The two girls decided to talk to Marlene's father as soon as possible. They were anxious to get everything ready as soon as possible.

Marlene invited Lourdes to go to the company together, and as soon as they arrived at the office, they immediately went to talk to João Alberto, who was very receptive and interested in their project. Despite having developed a deep dependence on his daughter in business, the Fiorucci patriarch understood that Marlene was trying to build her own path and her little daughter's future.

João Alberto wanted to deal personally with the owner of the property to try to negotiate the rental. Marlene and Lourdes accepted the businessman's conditions and, together, they went to the property.

During the meeting with the landlord, the two girls explained that the place needed a lot of renovation, so after a lot of negotiation, he agreed to lower the rent for one year. The contract was then closed.

A few days later, the renovation was started. Marlene had a good taste for decoration and dedicated herself to choosing the furniture, paints and some decoration pieces to create a cozy and refined environment for the atelier. For several weeks, the partners worked hard to make the place look as planned. The girls chose the name Studio das Marias, and a richly crafted plaque was hung on the front of the property.

The opening party was a success, because the ideas that Lourdes brought from Europe made the place unique. There were almost no ateliers of that magnitude.

Soon after the inauguration of the space, the orders began to arrive. Lourdes designed, cut and made the pieces, and Marlene took care of the administration. When the orders began to multiply, the two women decided to hire a helper, and Deise was chosen. The girl was very capable and showed great interest in advancing professionally.

***

It had been a few weeks have since the opening of the Atelier das Marias, and winter had arrived strongly in the city. The temperature had dropped a lot and the carioca upper class needed to renew their wardrobes. As a result, there was no more room in the studio for so many orders.

One afternoon, while working hard, the partners were talking:

– Marlene, I don't think we can handle it. It is only the three of us, and we have a lot of orders. There are so many details.

– Lourdes, we can hire one more helper with a little more experience. Do you think we should put an ad in the newspaper or look for someone through a referral?

– I think it had better be if it's someone we know.

Deise, knowing that Marlene and Lourdes were looking for a helper, indicated her aunt Rosângela. The partners liked the woman, because, besides being a seamstress, she was also an embroiderer. Without wasting any time, Marlene prepared all the paperwork to hire Rosângela, who was overjoyed. And so, the atelier evolved and grew day by day.

***

One afternoon, a young woman came into the atelier and began talking to Lourdes.

– Good afternoon, I need a winter dress – and she began to look at the ready-made coats that were on display. The girl was so enchanted by the pieces that she asked Lourdes to make her a coat as well. What beautiful pieces! I must bring my mother here. She will go crazy.

– Excuse me, what is your name?

– Renata.

– Welcome, Renata! My name is Lourdes. I'm the atelier stylist.

In the meantime, Marlene came in, bringing the fabrics she had bought and, when she ran into Renata, she asked:

– Wow, aren't you Renata, Paulo José's sister?

– Yes, that's me! How are you? It has been a long time since I've seen you. You're Marlene, right? How are things going?

– Yes, I'm Marlene. I'm fine! I'm a partner in this atelier.

– Marlene, I am sorry if I'm being inconvenient, but we overheard what happened to you. You know how it is... people talk. Well, I don't know if you are aware, but, around the same time, my brother was attacked, so we decided to stay away from social life for a while. Paulo José went to the interior to take care of my dad's farm, but he is already returning to Rio de Janeiro, because we sold the property. He will help our father in the family business.

– I am happy to hear that you are both doing well. And your brother is married yet?

– Not at all, Marlene. He is afraid of wedding rings. Mom and I would love to see him married, but so far, he has not wanted to get marriage. My father has been very ill, so we decided to sell the farm, and Paulo José will be closer to the family.

– And you, Renata? Did you get married?

– Not yet. I am engaged to Marcos, and plan to get married next year. We ended up buying a beautiful house, but it required a lot of structural renovations and delayed our marriage a lot. So, we decided to do everything calmly, to furnish the house without haste. Marcos is wonderful and helps me a lot with my family. And you, Marlene, are you already married?

– No. I had a daughter. After all the tragedy, I didn't have the courage to face another relationship. My life is reduced to my work, my house, my daughter and my parents.

– Marlene, I would like to meet your daughter! We must have coffee together. My mother will be very happy to know that we met again.

– That's fine with me. Bring your mother here to meet the atelier.

– Of course! Like I told you, my mother will go crazy with the pieces you have here! She loves to buy clothes – and she laughed.

– Renata, excuse me if I'm being indiscreet, but what happened to your father?

– He underwent surgery in which two hernias were removed. After the operation, my father had post–operative complications. We thought he wouldn't survive, and, after that, Dad was never the same again.

– Wow, how sad! Mr. Dionísio was always so strong.

– Yes, Marlene, my father was always very well disposed. He solved many complex cases, bought a farm and made many deals to invest what he had earned in law practice. My father is my everything!

At that moment, Renata began to cry, and Marlene hugged her tenderly and said:

– Calm down, Renata, he will be that strong man again.

– Wow, here I am crying and you, who have been through so many problems, are so strong, comforting me! I am sorry, Marlene.

– Renata, we are in this life to learn, and we must walk with God in front of us.

The two women said goodbye, and Renata left.

Marlene then vented to her partner.

– Lourdes, my God, I have to tell you something, but I am ashamed to recall this story after so much time.

– My God, Marlene! We're friends. Do you think I would judge you for anything?

– No, I know you don't. Anyway... when I was dating Júlio, we had a fight, nothing serious, just a lovers' quarrel... soon after this discussion I went to a party, met some of Júlio's friends and drank too much, something I had never done before. Then, I ended up... oh my God, how can I say this? Well... I gave myself to one of his friends: Paulo José. It was only once, and I never talked to him about what happened between us. I believe that he also felt guilty for betraying his friend. I know that my daughter is Júlio's – of that I have no doubt –, but I suspect that Júlio found out about this double betrayal and tried to kill Paulo José.

Marlene paused before continuing:

– Things became unresolved between those involved. When I learned that Júlio was the one who ordered my kidnapping, I was devastated. Besides, I never knew what he intended to do with me, what he would do with me. Maybe he trying to kill me, I don't know. I suspect that he tried to kill Paulo José.

– Do you think he would be able to do that?

– Lourdes, Júlio was able to send two men to kidnap me, to hold me captive, knowing that I was carrying his child in my womb. Do you think he would not be able to shoot his friend, knowing that he betrayed his trust? I really believe that Júlio was responsible for the attack and that Paulo José knew about it, but he did not want to hand his friend over to the police because he felt guilty about it.

– Marlene, I am shocked! I had no idea about all this!

– I am ashamed of my past and of my weaknesses, Lourdes....

– Honey, I can't even imagine what you have been going through all that time, keeping this secret under lock and key, unable to open to anyone.

– Really, it was all very sad, Lourdes. My daughter was born because God and the spiritual world allowed it.

– Marlene, you need to remake your life, get married, start a family, and maybe even have more children.

– My friend, I can't even imagine resuming my love life. I am very afraid, and, besides, I am no longer alone. After Maria Helena's birth, I started to foresee having a relationship with someone and exposing my daughter. I think mainly of my parents because they suffered a lot because of my mistakes. I still can't forgive myself for everything I did.

– Marlene, life is made of mistakes and successes. If you acted that way, it's because you didn't know any other way to handle the situation. Don't judge yourself so harshly. You have changed and today you take care of your daughter and your parents with great care. You are more mature now. Open your heart and allow happiness to dwell in your life. Give love a new chance.

Lourdes' words went deep into Marlene's soul. The girl was right. She had made a mistake, but she had learned her lesson. From now on, everything would be different.

CHAPTER 15

A few days had passed since the last events and Marlene kept on trying to take care of her family. The girl was committed to raising Maria Helena, helping her daughter to develop good moral values so that, in the future, she would become a fair person with good character. Marlene, each day, understood that living on Earth was a gift from God, an opportunity to improve her spirit and to seek inner growth, and that the adversities, the illnesses, the problems that she encountered and would still encounter along her path were like lessons for her learning. It was hard to accept the afflictions, but with faith in God, Marlene would manage to make the burden lighter.

That morning, while the family was eating, Marlene noticed that, lately, her father had been complaining of constant tiredness. It seemed to her that João Alberto had lost the will to live and the joy of playing with his granddaughter.

Due to João Alberto's growing apathy and since Marlene was leaving the company – because she had decided to dedicate herself exclusively to her atelier – Raul had to take a more active role in the company, since Carlos, the boy's father, was quite overwhelmed by his partner's absence. In this way, day by day, Raul distanced more and more from his dream of living in Portugal, which caused a crisis in his relationship with his boyfriend. Roberto's demands became constant, because he did not understand that Raul loved him, but could not turn his back on his father.

In an attempt to resolve the situation, Raul calls Roberto for a conversation to think together about a solution.

– Roberto, I love you very much and believe me, I do not intend to give up our plans. Understand that I am facing a dilemma now, because I can't abandon my father at such a difficult time, but I also do not want to hurt you. If you want to go to Portugal alone and start something there, of course I'll suffer, but I'll understand your decision.

Roberto did not know what to say to his companion, so he just shut up. After a few moments he said that he needed to think about everything that was happening and that it was better for the two of them to stay apart for a while.

Raul did not expect that reaction from his partner and, very sad, looked for Marlene to unburden himself and ask for her help. He was lost and did not imagine that Roberto would be so insensitive to the point of not putting himself in his place to find a solution to the situation together.

– Marlene, I really need your help! I am completely lost.

– What happened, Raul?

– You know that your father is not well and that my father no longer enjoys the same vitality. Faced with this situation, I can't abandon everything. Roberto often doesn't seem to understand the dilemma I'm going through and, lately we have been arguing a lot, which has hindered our relationship. I told him that, if he wanted, he could go to Portugal, which was very difficult for me, because my heart is broken.

– Calm down, Raul. I'm sure Roberto won't go anywhere without you.

– But, Marlene, I don't have the right to ask him to stay. I am feeling very bad about this situation, and I feel sorry for him, who also has so many dreams and is so dedicated. Sometimes, I keep wondering what the future of our relationship will be. We plan to live together; however, I know that here it will be impossible because our family will not accept it. In Portugal, everything would be easier.

– Raul, wait for his decision before you suffer. I believe that Roberto will understand your problems and will help you through this difficult time. You are young and you are not giving up on your dreams, you are just putting them off a little.

– Will it work? Will he accept to stay here for a while longer?

– I think so! And, if I were you, I would rent a property and live on my own. You need to earn your freedom, get out of your parents' house. I would like to do the same, but I have Maria Helena. Since I must go out to work, she is in the care of my mother, who has helped me a lot.

– You are right, Marlene. I really need a path, to make some changes in my life, and living alone might be a good idea. Moving to a neighborhood where nobody knows me or Roberto. But... what should I do? I am afraid because I have already told him about going to Portugal and making his life alone.

Thoughtful, Raul left after talking to Marlene. Intimately, the boy wondered: "What should I do? Could it be that Roberto does not love me anymore?" Unfortunately, some people, trapped in imaginary dramas, transform their own existence into an ordeal and suffer unnecessary afflictions, believing that they will only be happy with someone else, but only true love brings happiness and frees the human being from illusions. Raul still needed to learn a lot about the meaning of love, because only in this way, he would free himself from the fears and anxieties that dwelt in his tormented soul.

✱ ✱ ✱

Alone in her atelier, Marlene thought about the conversation she had had with her friend. The girl was very worried, because Raul and Roberto were her best friends, and she did not want anything to spoil the relationship between the two boys, even because she knew the love that existed between them.

After much thought, she decided to call Roberto and make an appointment for them to talk about it. Who knows, maybe he would listen to her arguments and try to better understand his partner?

Marlene and Roberto met in a coffee shop near the girl's atelier, and after the greetings, she started on the subject she needed to discuss with the boy.

– Roberto, excuse me... I don't want to invade your life or Raul's, but I am very worried. He came to me out and told me about the last conversation you had.

Seeing that Roberto was paying attention to what she was saying, Marlene paused and continued:

– He is in a very bad way, because he loves you very much and has the best intentions towards you. Raul would like to live with you, to share your lives, but he knows that it would be very difficult here, because both of your families would not accept it. So, I gave him the idea of renting a property and moving to his own corner because, that way, things would be easier. I know you are tired of hiding the relationship and that you also have a dream of starting a business... but, Roberto, it can all happen here! And I can help you. And I have a lot of ideas, huh!

– Marlene, I keep thinking... how long will all this be like? I can't even have a life with the one I truly love, because I know Raul couldn't leave his parents. I also have my parents and I know that they would never accept our relationship, so only in Portugal will we be free to live our love. I know you are right and that I may be being selfish, so I have decided to take a break. I don't want to hurt Raul. I thought I would take a trip by myself to relax and rest my mind.

– I think it would be good for you to be apart for a while, so that you can reflect on all these issues. Who knows, maybe a good idea that will please both of you won't come up? Talk to him.

– I am going to talk to him on the weekend. I plan to invite him for coffee and tell him that I will be making this trip to think a little more about the two of us. I believe this is the way. Thank you, Marlene, for being such a wonderful person and for always trying to help us with all this affection.

– I am grateful for the opportunity to have you as friends and brothers. You know how important you are to my daughter.

– Ah, we love you very much, darling.

Roberto said goodbye, and Marlene stayed a little longer in the coffee shop, thinking about everything they have talked about. The girl was heartbroken because she knew the situation was very complicated, but she prayed and put her worries in God's hands. He would show Raul and Roberto the right path.

✳ ✳ ✳

The weekend went by quickly and on Monday morning Marlene decided to arrive at the atelier earlier, because she had prepared a cost report and would like to discuss some actions with her partner. Amused by this task, the girl was surprised by Raul's visit. – Good morning, Marlene!

– Hello, Raul! What good winds bring you early?

– Actually, they are not good winds, but my anguish. There are times that I don't even know what to do. I feel a chill in my stomach every time I think about Roberto. It's as if I'm losing him with each passing day.

– Calm down, Raul. I talked to Roberto. He told me that he will be taking a trip soon to think about everything that is going on. I am sure that, like you, he is very unhappy about this whole situation, because he would very much like for you to assume the relationship. Roberto, however, knows that that would be impossible here.

– Ah, Marlene, he came to talk to me about the trip, but I found him so cold and distant, I'm afraid. What if he concludes that he should start his life all over again far away from here?

– Raul, you need to trust this love. I know that Roberto loves you very much.

– Yes, you are right. I can no longer torture myself like this, because it's doing me a lot of harm. I'm going to rethink my life. Besides, I also feel that my father is not very well, and I won't abandon him at this time. It would be inhuman.

– I am here to support you in whatever you need, Raul. If, for the time being, it is impossible to move to another country, at least think about renting an apartment and gaining your independence. I am sure that a space of your own, a home, will be better for the future of your relationship.

The boy listened to Marlene, but his thoughts were far away. Suddenly, he asked his friend:

– Marlene, what do you think about us going to the Spiritist center? I feel so calm there, even though I don't receive messages. Besides, I need some passes. I feel very heavy.

– Sure, we will! What do you say we call Roberto? Has he already traveled?

– No! I need to go alone! Can you come with me?

– I'll talk to Mrs. Mercedes, and we'll go there.

– Great! Shall I pick you up here at the atelier or at your place, at the end of the day?

– It can be at home. I want to take a shower before I go.

✽ ✽ ✽

The day went on with no news and, at dusk, Raul stopped by Marlene's house. From there, the two went to Mercedes' Spiritist Center.

The place was all lit up and people were slowly arriving and settling down on the rows of white chairs, keeping themselves in prayer. A soft scent of roses flooded the room, which was painted in light colors, and in the background, a soft melody harmonized the space. At the end of the sessions, a group of mediums distributed the messages received through psychography.

The center's leader started the session by reading of an excerpt from The Gospel According to Spiritualism, and after the explanations about the text read, Raul and Marlene received a collective pass to balance their energies.

One of the mediums in the group was a young girl, who appeared to be 23 years old. Sitting at a table with some sheets of paper in front of her, she had just received a message from a young man, whose mother sitting in one of the rows of white chairs, was very emotional.

Reinaldo, the boy who communicated through the medium had died three years ago in an accident. He and Fabio, a friend, had gone to a graduation party and had drunk too much. Fabio, who was driving the vehicle at high speed, lost control of the car on a curve and crashed into a pole. The driver died on the spot and Reinaldo remained in a coma for 15 days until he died.

Marlene was next to Reinaldo's mother when the lady received the message. Soon after, the medium Simone took a deep breath and went into a trance. The girl lowered her head, put her hands on the table and began to cry, saying:

– Forgive me!

She was whispering and repeating repeatedly the request:

– Forgive me! Forgive me!

At that instant, Simone pulled out the paper in front of her and began to write messily.

Raul, who was watching the whole scene, was staring at the medium. Curious, he commented to Marlene:

– Wow, I wonder who is asking so much for someone's forgiveness?

– It must be someone who is here. I wonder if it was some husband's betrayal.

Raul started laughing at the way Marlene had referred to the case and little did the girl know that it was Júlio who had come there desperate to communicate. The boy was very weak and with a lot of effort managed to transmit the message he wanted, whose content Marlene would know at the end of the session.

Before Raul could answer Marlene, an assistant from the center asked the boy to accompany him because he needed spiritual help.

At the end of the session, the center leader, in possession of the messages, had the mission of addressing them to their proper recipients, calling each one by name. When Marlene's name was pronounced, the girl began to feel a palpitation and her hands became cold.

With the sheet of paper in her hands, Marlene could not contain her emotion as she read the few words forwarded to her.

"Marlene, please forgive me, I am in a very ill and I need your help! I know you have a good heart, and that Maria Helena is my daughter. I can hardly stand up. I am very weak, but I need your forgiveness."

By the end of the reading, the girl was in tears. Marlene finally concluded that the laws that govern destiny are perfect and that we are all eternal spirits seeking to improve ourselves each day on Earth. Between tears she understood that death is only a change in dimension but that we are still alive on the other side, masters of our feelings and slaves to our inclinations.

Later, when she was home, Marlene reread the letter several times and began to pray. The girl wanted to forgive Júlio, but mistakenly asked him to stay away from her and Maria Helena. Marlene was not yet ready to let go of all the resentment she had for Júlio.

Calmer, the girl called her mother and told her everything that had happened in the session and how shaken she was. Emília then asked her daughter to accept the adversities as life lessons and to forgive Júlio without asking for anything in return. The woman felt that Marlene still harbored feelings of resentment toward her former boyfriend.

– Mom, I know that I need to forgive Júlio, but it's all so difficult. He was very cruel and didn't even think about the child I was carrying. A child that was his daughter! That man locked me up in a shack in the middle of nowhere, pregnant. I could have lost my daughter! It's not so easy to forgive something like that, mother. Besides, I'm sure he also tried to kill Paulo José. Do you think that just the fact of forgiving him will keep him away from me and Maria Helena?

– I'm sure he would free himself and be at peace, my daughter! Why don't you go back to the center and ask for guidance? They will help you, darling.

– I'm going to talk to Mrs. Mercedes. I didn't want to bother her, but I know you're right. I really need help, and so does Júlio. I am really afraid that he will get close to Maria Helena and harm her.

The next day, Marlene went to Mercedes and was instructed by the kind lady to take some courses to learn a little more about spirituality and to get rid of negative feelings. Study, when well oriented, is the gateway to a balanced life.

Remembering her friend Marlene asked for permission to take Raul to the courses, which was promptly authorized by Mercedes, because it is the needs that move men to assume the changes and seek the long-awaited time of evolution. To do so, it is necessary to open our minds and understand how wise the laws of life are, that make available all the resources for our learning.

CHAPTER 16

Time passes quickly for those who work hard and keep their minds active, cultivating edifying thoughts. During this period, Júlio never again had contact with Marlene, who together with Raul, continued to study the spiritual life. Little by little, they both learned about the need for forgiveness, the importance of having good feelings and the importance of always being connected to spirituality through prayer. During this process, Marlene became more optimistic and, little by little, she got rid of resentment, pain and fear, for these feelings had been acting negatively on the girl's spirit for a long time, transforming her into a sad and empty person.

The classes at the Spiritist Center gave Raul strength to overcome many things, especially Roberto's decision to travel to Portugal. After the shock of the news the boy decided to think about himself for a while and finally moved from his parents' house to an apartment he rented downtown. However, the anxiety for Roberto's return persisted, even though he did not know if their relationship would have a future. The longing was very big.

In Portugal, Roberto was taking some courses related to his field. The boy also missed Raul but was happy to have left Brazil. Each one, respecting his free will, was conquering his objectives and executing his life projects.

After a few months, Roberto sent a letter to his companion saying that he did not know yet when he would return, which generated an avalanche of feelings in Raul, who was emotionally unstable at the time. He believed that with this prolonged absence, Roberto intended to punish him for not having moved with him to Europe, thus oscillating between reason and disturbance.

Marlene, a devoted friend, was present in all of Raul's moments of crisis, and their friendship grew every day. The boy, wanting company, always invited Marlene and Maria Helena to spend the weekend at his house, so he could cheat the sadness and enjoy more time with his goddaughter.

On one of those weekends, Raul and Marlene took Maria Helena to the park and then to a very elegant tea house that the three of them loved to go to. Marlene always showed genuine joy in seeing him smile and give Maria Helena so much affection.

At the tea house, after twenty minutes of their arrival, Marlene saw two well-dressed girls enter the room. One of them was Renata, Paulo José's sister. The newcomer did not see Marlene who approached saying:

– What a surprise, Renata!

– Marlene! Wow! You here in the center of town! What a nice surprise!

– I'm here with Raul, my daughter's godfather. I brought her to see him and to walk around a little. And you? Did you come for a walk too?

– Yes! This is my friend Márcia, an excellent psychiatrist. We came for a walk and I'm very happy to meet you, because I'm having a party at my house for my mother's birthday, and I'd love to have you there. I'm sure Mom will be very happy to see you. We will even go to your atelier to make our dresses.

– It will be a pleasure, Renata. When will the party be? I'll ask Lourdes to make a beautiful dress for your mother. It will be my birthday present.

– No, no, Marlene! We make it a point to pay because it's your job. I would just like to count on your presence. And I also invite Raul and Lourdes. We have already started the preparations because the party will be in a month and a half from now.

– No problem. When can you go to the atelier?

– I will arrange it with mom, but it will be soon. I promise.

The two girls had tea together and then said goodbye. Renata loved meeting Maria Helena. The girl had fallen in love with the beauty of the girl who was a very affectionate child.

During the way back home, Raul and Marlene talked.

– Oh, Raul, I got a chill in my stomach. You knew that Paulo José will be there, didn't you? How am I going to face him after all?

– Marlene, you must go, after all, it's been so long.

– Raul, I have never talked about it with you, but at the time I was dating Júlio, I already had feelings for Paulo José.

I don't know to this day if it was just a very strong attraction or something else...all I know is that the night I gave myself to him, I felt like I was floating.

– You have surprised me now!

– Even I surprise myself sometimes my friend. Believe me!

– So, it wasn't really alcohol that made you surrender to Paulo José's arms, was it?

– I had never drunk before in my life, my friend. It was a completely unusual situation for me. I was fighting with Júlio and had heard the most profound barbarisms from him. After this fight, I went to a party of my father's friends and ended up meeting Paulo José there. We frequented practically the same circles. Since I was dating Júlio, he came over to greet me and we chatted. That night I had several glasses of champagne. I was very hurt... Anyway, during the conversation Paulo José invited me to walk a little, to get some air, and that was when things happened between us. He kissed me passionately and the only thing I know is that I gave myself body and soul to him that night.

– Honey, have you ever considered the possibility that you have a story to live with Paulo José?

– Wow, Raul, I can't imagine that! Out of respect for Júlio, I'm sure he will never want me. And another thing! His parents would never accept me as their daughter–in–law, after all, I had a daughter with another man. Don't you know how society works, my friend? And another thing! I'll only go to that party if you and Lourdes accompany me. My God, why have I been so weak and gave myself to Paulo José?

– Marlene, stop punishing yourself for that! You didn't commit any crime! Stop playing society's game! Have you realized what you're doing? You just told me that when you were dating Júlio you already had feelings for Paulo José. Maybe you still have something to live for. Understand once and for all that everything in life is right, my friend. Everything is right. Get into in your head once and for all. You need to move on with your life because you have the right to be happy. And if this story must happen, it will happen. And I will tell you one more thing: if Roberto takes a long time to come back, I will move on with my life! That is what I have learned in the courses at the center. We are not victims and every day we reap what we sow. We must give a chance to the new and that's what I'm going to do, Marlene!

– Wow, Raul, I am amazed! Would you have the courage to relate to someone else?

– Of course! I am not abandoning Roberto with this decision, but I understand that he has the right to make his own choices. I have to respect the free will of the person I love. I'm sorry, but I can't stop in time and dwell on this pain.

– I don't even know what to tell you, my friend. Maybe because I like you both so much, I was a bit stunned by what you just told me, but I know you are right. I also need to review my concepts and remake my life. My fear, in fact, is of bringing someone into my daughter's life who doesn't love her. I know that I should not look for a father for her, but I need someone who will respect her.

– I will always be by your side and by Maria Helena's side, my dear. Know that I will protect my goddaughter like a father. I can tell you that the most important person in my life, the one who makes me want to wake up every day and live, is Maria Helena.

– Raul, you are everything to her. Thank you, my friend.

The boy was thrilled with so much affection and, to disguise the commotion, he changed the subject:

– Marlene, if you are really going to Paulo José's mother's party, ask Lourdes to design you a beautiful dress. I want to see you looking stunning! If Renata invited you, it's because she wants you to come.

– I don't have the courage to go to this party alone. I'll only go if you and Lourdes accompany me.

Raul started to laugh.

– Do I go on the offer?

– Yes! You are going on the offer and handsome. Please, Raul.

– Hum, I'm sensing that you really want to see Paulo José...Is there something very strong left in your heart?

– I'm really afraid of meeting him again, but it's silly of me. I am sure that he won't even remember me, because a long time has passed. Paulo José must have already met someone else, because he was a very attractive man, coveted and popular man among women. He must not be short of suitors.

– Well, we'll go to the party and see if there's still anything left between the two of you.

– I even wanted to believe that, but it's better not to get my hopes up. I think my needy side is imagining things. Although I have drunk a few glasses of champagne, my body was awake that night and I still have memories of everything that happened.

Raul smiled. Suddenly, the boy was excited about Marlene's invitation and began to imagine what he would wear to the party.

– I want to go with my new suit! I need something to bring me joy and I know that this party promises!

Cheerful and given to the joy of that moment, the two friends continued to make plans for the party.

✳ ✳ ✳

A few days later, Renata and Eunice went to Marlene and Lourdes' atelier to have measurements taken. Marlene was there and with her good taste, presented several ideas for her customers. Mother and daughter chose simple but sophisticated model and Lourdes began to design the dresses.

Marlene also wanted to make a good impression, because deep down, with her womanly vanity, she wanted to be noticed by Paulo José. Would he still find her attractive after so many years? The girl asked Lourdes to design an elegant dress for her and spared no resources in acquiring a beautiful blue lace that would be used for the outfit. After so many years and so much suffering, Marlene was willing to reconnect with the woman she had once been.

✳ ✳ ✳

Excited with the preparations for the party, everyone did not even see time passing and when they least expected it, the big date arrived.

Marlene was beside herself with anxiety. In the morning, at the atelier, she had confided to Lourdes that she had not been able to sleep the day before the event and that she would go to the beauty salon after resolving some pending issues. The girl wanted to look impeccable for the party.

After getting her hair and makeup done at the salon, Marlene returned home. She was agitated and checked several times the dress, shoes and jewelry she would wear to the party. Next to her daughter, Emília only observed the change in the girl's behavior and thought: "Marlene is not acting natural. Could it be that she is acting this way because she will meet Paulo José again?"

When she returned home after the days of captivity and hospitalization, Marlene decided to tell her mother everything that had happened with her up that moment. She told her about the fight with Júlio, the strong attraction she felt for Paulo José, the night she gave herself to the boy and the pregnancy. At the time, Emília, still very attached to the dictates of society, had difficulty understanding all those situations that her daughter had confided to her, but as time went by her motherly heart calmed down.

Emília did not have any negative feelings towards Paulo José; she just did not want her daughter to be hurt again. Fearful, she said a heartfelt prayer, knowing that the good spirits of light would watch over Marlene.

Night finally dawned in all its splendor. The stars illuminated the city, and a soft breeze cooled the spring climate. Raul had arranged to pick Marlene up at her place of residence and from there they went to Lourdes' house.

The boy arrived punctually at the agreed time and was welcomed by Emília, who led him to the living room to wait for his friend.

When the girl came down the stairs, everyone in the room fell silent because she was simply stunning. All around her, the girl had an illuminated aura that radiated brightness throughout the room. It was the happiness that slowly returned to that spirit that had suffered after her bad choices.

Proud of his friend, Raul said that she would be the most beautiful woman at the party.

– Marlene, you look gorgeous. Your dress is simply wonderful. I don't know what it really is, but I see a glow in you. Something that comes from inside, from the height of your heart. It must be because you are excited for the party.

Marlene just smiled and hurried her friend because she didn't want to be late to the party. The two friends then said goodbye to Emília and left in the direction of happiness.

✳ ✳ ✳

When Raul, Marlene and Lourdes arrived at the party at Renata's house, they saw several cars and many people in the place. Everything had been carefully prepared to receive the guests. The luxurious residence boasted all the class and refinement of its owners.

The three friends commented without containing their surprise:

– Wow, how many people!

– My God, I didn't imagine it would be such a revelry!

Lourdes and Marlene were ecstatically contemplating all the details that made up that dream scenario, when they heard Raul's comment:

– Will I find my prince at this party? – asked the boy.

– Stop Raul! Your prince's name is Roberto! – Marlene scolded her friend.

– I don't know, but I think the distance has made Roberto forget me. So, if someone arouses my interest I will flirt yes!

Without wasting any time, the three of them entered the richly decorated room and greeted Eunice and Renata, who showed genuine satisfaction at seeing them there. Soon after, they were led to a table where a plaque with their name was set with fine cutlery, delicate glasses and beautiful flower arrangements. Everything had been chosen to meet the taste of the most demanding.

The orchestra played a harmonious melody that brightened the atmosphere and rocked the arrival of the guests. Gradually the rich salon began to be filled with the finest and most elegant members of Rio de Janeiro's upper class.

Disguisedly, Marlene ran her eyes around the room but had not yet seen Paulo José. Without containing her impulses and overcome by an indefinable uneasiness, the girl felt her heart almost bursting out of her mouth.

After a few minutes, Marlene finally spotted Paulo José entering the room next to a girl of rare beauty. The couple sat at another table next to Marlene and her friends.

It did not take long for Paulo José to spot Marlene, but he did not go to the table where she was sitting. This caused great sadness to the girl, who hoped that he had not forgotten her.

Sitting next to Marlene, Raul realized the whole situation and tried to console her friend.

– Calm down, Marlene, you can't be so tense. I can see the anguish in your eyes. Let's have a glass of champagne to relax so you can enjoy the party more. Look how many beautiful men there are here! What do you think, Lourdes?

– You're terrible, Raul. No one is sad around you! I loved that idea of enjoying the party and having a glass of champagne.

– I wonder if that girl is his girlfriend. How beautiful she is! – Marlene asked.

– We'll soon find out! When we say hello, put on your prettiest face!

– Raul, I am trembling. How silly I am... Paulo José has every right to date, to build a family, after all, it was just one night. Nothing more serious happened between us and...

– Calm down, Marlene! We still don't know who the girl is! My God, woman!

– Am I jealous? What's going on with me?

– There's a volcano erupting inside. You're discovering how much you love him.

– Will he ignore me, Raul?

– I'm sure he'll come to greet you. What do you think, Lourdes?

– I realize he can't take his eye off here, and it's not me he's looking at, is it?!

– Raul, get another glass of champagne! Let's toast!

– Sure, Marlene! And speaking of toasting, have you seen that guy sitting there with two friends? He's already looked at me a little! – said Raul, with a good laugh to lighten the mood.

At that moment, even Marlene surrendered to her friend's laughter and decided to enjoy the evening.

The party was lively, while Dionísio and Eunice, the hosts, went around greeting everyone present. Renata went to the table where Marlene was.

– Are you enjoying the party?

– Everything is wonderful, Renata. We love the decoration, everything is perfect!

– Marlene, have you already talked to Paulo José?

– No, I was a little embarrassed because he has a company. I don't want to be inconvenient.

– That girl is our cousin, my mother's sister's daughter. Her name is Maristela. She's a lovely person. My brother is keeping her company until my aunt arrives. My cousin is spending a few days here at home. She's like a sister to us.

At that moment, Marlene's eyes sparkled with joy. "So, Paulo José is not dating anyone? Is there hope for us?" the girl wondered.

Suddenly, the orchestra began to play romantic music, awakening in the couples the desire to dance, and the room came alive. Joy was the keynote of that environment.

– Shall we dance, my friend? It's not possible that you made such a beautiful dress and asked for a wonderful hairstyle to spend the whole night sitting down, is it? – Raul invited.

– I am ashamed, Raul.

– It is okay. In a little while, that shame will disappear. I will dance with Lourdes then.

– You can go. I will be here watching.

Marlene remained seated at the table, watching the couple of friends who were whirling around the room, and didn't notice Paulo José walking towards her.

– Hello, Marlene. Long time no sees! How beautiful you look! May I sit here and keep you company?

Marlene's heart did not fit inside her chest. Emotional, the girl could barely answer the boy:

– Of course! It'll be a pleasure! – she stammered.

Paulo José pretended not to notice the girl's nervousness and asked:

– Will you join me in a glass of champagne?

– I don't know if I should... I'm a little dizzy, as I've had a few glasses. But that's okay... just one more to go with you.

They then engaged in a lively conversation. At a certain moment, Marlene tried to talk about the past, but Paulo José asked her not to talk about it, because this was a time for joy.

– Marlene, let's enjoy the party. I would just like to enjoy your company. The past is behind us.

– Sorry, you are absolute right. We should just have fun – Marlene retracted.

– Shall we dance? – proposed Paulo José.

– I don't dance very well...

– But I can lead you. I am an excellent dancer!

– So... – Marlene replied, letting herself be involved in the moment.

In the distance, Paulo José's parents followed the couple, whirling around the room. Dionísio was not happy with that approach.

Still wrapped up in the magic of the moment, Marlene had noticed the sneaky glances directed at her. The girl was then overcome by an unpleasant feeling, but soon recovered and surrendered to the music.

The party went on and everything was normal. Later, when most of the guests had already left, Marlene left the place exhausted, wanting only to return home.

That night, it was very difficult for Marlene to get to sleep, because she thought about Paulo José the whole night.

The next day, Marlene woke up early and decided that, before going to the atelier, she would stop by the company to meet Raul.

After greeting the receptionist, the girl went to her friend's office.

– Hi, Raul, good morning! How are you? Did you like the party?

– I loved it, dear! I had a great time! I just woke up with a bit of a headache, but I think this is because I had a little too much champagne. I know that your head must be spinning because I could see that Paulo José and you can still have a beautiful story.

– I can't stop thinking about him, but I'm not going to look for him, Raul. I still feel ashamed for everything that happened in the past.

– Marlene, may God's will be done. You certainly still have something to live out together, and I know he will look for you yet. Time will show us.

– He really wanted to give myself that chance, to live a great love, but he will not want me with a daughter. Besides, from what I understand, his family would not accept me.

Raul and Marlene talked for a while and then said goodbye, because they had a lot of work to do.

***

And so, in this confusion of feelings that Marlene was experiencing, two months went by without the girl and Paulo José ever meeting again.

One night, Marlene dreamed about Júlio who said to her: "Marlene, go on with your life. I only ask that you forgive me, for I am very sorry. Take care of our daughter. I know I don't deserve your forgiveness, but I also know that you are a very good person and, who knows, one day, you may forgive me..."

Júlio hugged Marlene, who woke up for a moment and then went back to sleep.

In the morning, Marlene got up and remembered in detail her dream, which had distressed her during the day. It was a very real dream, and since she was studying the Spiritist doctrine, she understood that it was really an encounter. The girl had really been with Júlio, and he had asked her for forgiveness.

Back to the atelier, Marlene told the dream to Lourdes, who spoke words of comfort to her.

In the late afternoon, when Marlene was getting ready to go home, Paulo José entered the atelier. The girl was overcome by an intense wave of emotion.

–Wow! What a surprise to see you here! Have a seat! Would you like some coffee?

– No, thank you. I'd like to have coffee with you, but somewhere else. Would you have some time for that?

– If you can wait a bit... I was just getting ready to leave.

– Of course. I wait for you to finish what you must do. Minutes later, Marlene and Paulo José left the atelier for a charming café that the girl indicated.

The place, whose decoration was reminiscent of Parisian cafeterias, was simple but tasteful. When they entered, Paulo José looked for a table farther away so they could talk calmly. In a gallant manner, he pulled out a chair for Marlene and invited her to sit down. After the waiter took their order, Paulo José introduced the subject that had led him to look for the girl.

After the silence of all those years, Paulo José was resolute. They had to talk about everything that had happened. Marlene's eyes filled with tears. The moment of truth had arrived. From now on, if the relationship was to move forward, it was necessary that all the old problems be solved.

The two talked about Júlio and about the boy's actions. Paulo José showed genuine interest in Marlene's life over the past few years and wanted to know if the girl was engaged to anyone.

– No, I am alone. During all this time, I did not have the courage to be with anyone else. I was very traumatized by everything Júlio did to me, and I had a hard time trusting a man again. And you?

– I am also alone. I had someone, but it didn't work out. I didn't love her. Marlene, could we meet again? I would like to talk more to you.

– It will be a pleasure to be by your side – she smiled shyly.

From that day on, there were many more meetings between Paulo José and Marlene. Each day, they were more involved. It was a pure feeling, forged by the maturity they had acquired because of past events. There were no more obstacles between them, so the inevitable happened.

One day, taking advantage of the magic of the moment, Paulo José asked Marlene to date, and the girl, overcome with emotion and profound happiness, promptly accepted his proposal.

– I accept, my love! You don't know how long I have waited for this. How long my heart has waited for this moment.

– It wasn't just one night for me, Marlene. I just didn't have the time or the opportunity to tell you that before. I had a guilty conscience for having betrayed Júlio's trust, but I also couldn't deny to myself that that night had moved me. That having you in my arms had marked me.

– For a long time, I blamed myself for giving in to weakness, but I understand that everything in life has a reason, dear. Maybe, if things had not happened the way they did, we would not be here together. So, let's look to the future, okay? All is all right in life.

The two kissed passionately, but suddenly Marlene's eyes were filled with a haze of anguish.

– But... what if your family doesn't accept me, Paulo? How will we do? I have a daughter who is still small.

– Marlene, my decision has already been made, but rest assured, because I am sure that my parents will accept you. Besides, my sister likes you very much. And more! I'm going to talk to your parents to ask permission to date you.

– Oh, how kind of you! I only ask you to wait a little longer so that I can talk to them first. Later, I'll arrange a dinner at home so we can make our relationship official.

With their fingers intertwined and their eyes fixed on each other, the couple remained in a small talk. Later, when they said goodbye, Paulo José and Marlene were lighthearted and sure that from now on they would be very happy.

✲ ✲ ✲

The next day, Marlene used breakfast to talk to her parents about Paulo José's request to date her, which was not very well received by the girl's father.

Suspicious, João Alberto advised his daughter to slow down and not to give herself over to that relationship with an open heart.

– Dad, stay calm. I will be careful, but we want to try. He knows that I have a daughter and that she means everything to me.

João Alberto's reaction was protective. He cared about his daughter and did not want her to be disappointed again, so he was reticent. He had nothing against Paulo José.

The girl said goodbye to her family and headed back to the atelier, because she would have a busy day and had scheduled several meetings with new suppliers.

At the end of the day, after finishing work, Marlene met Paulo José at their favorite restaurant. After greeting each other with a passionate kiss, the two examined the menu and chose their dishes. The young man, always gallant, ordered a wine to accompany the delicious meal.

The conversation flowed pleasantly between the kindred souls, and the girl, in love, looked tenderly at the boy. Soft music enveloped the atmosphere.

Marlene took a sip of orange juice and said:

– I've already talked to my parents about us, dear. They invited you for dinner at our house. It's scheduled for next weekend, okay?

– Sure, it will be perfect!

The lovers continued exchanging confidences and making plans for the future. Wise in its lessons, life rewards its students with the conquest of happiness at the end of the test.

✳ ✳ ✳

On the appointed day, Paulo José, punctually, rang the doorbell of his girlfriend's house. In his hands he carried a bouquet of flowers for Emilia and a Port wine for João Alberto.

The young man was received with warmth and attention by Marlene's family, who looked beautiful in a burgundy satin dress that highlighted her fair complexion.

Reunited, they started a lively talk about trivial matters, and after a delicious meal offered by the hosts, Paulo José and the Marlene's family went to the living room to enjoy a delicious genipap liqueur.

Without further ado, Paulo José introduced the subject that had brought him there that night. Respectfully, the boy explained his intentions to Marlene and asked the girl's parents for their permission to date her. João Alberto and Emília promptly blessed their relationship and, happy with their union, proposed a toast to seal their commitment.

Marlene asked to be excused and soon after returned to the living room with Maria Helena, who was introduced to Paulo José. The boy could not hide his amazement for the beautiful child that showed a lot of love in her eyes. A little shy at first, Maria Helena soon loosened up and started a lively conversation with Paulo José, insisting on showing him the doll her grandmother had given her.

Sharing very pleasant moments, no one saw the time pass by. When he realized how late it was, Paulo José said goodbye and returned home, happy with the way things had turned out.

One morning, when the family was gathered for the morning meal, Paulo José decided to tell his parents about his affair.

The boy's mother showed joy at the news, but Dionísio, upon learning who the girl was, verbalized his displeasure:

– With so many beautiful girls out there, you decided to date one who already has a daughter, is a single mother? Especially with everything that has happened to you.

– Father, I love Marlene and I will raise her daughter as if she were my own.

– Well, my son, you are already the master of your life, but that saddens me very much. I don't agree with your conduct.

Paulo José felt saddened by his father's attitude, but he was sure of his decision. He loved Marlene with all the strength of his heart, as he had never loved any other woman, and nothing would stop them from being together.

A few days later, Paulo José invited Marlene and Maria Helena to his house for a snack. Mother and daughter were well received by Eunice, who was delighted with the beautiful and polite child, but Marlene astute noticed the contrariness stamped on Dionísio's face. Even though Renata tried to soften the situation, the atmosphere quickly became unpleasant, because a wave of harmful energies had formed in the environment.

After the snack, Paulo José decided to take Marlene and Maria Helena home, and on the way, they talked about Dionísio's behavior. He, however, did not mind his father's resistance in accepting the relationship, because he knew that little by little the patriarch would get used to the idea.

Intimately, Marlene was still very worried, because she knew how much Paulo José was attached to his father, but with the study at the Spiritist Center, she had learned to trust life and the determinations of the Spirituality.

✶✶✶

Nature is made of cycles that follow perfect and harmonic laws, according to the passage of time. This is what happens with our life that obeys a route drawn by our spirit, but that many times undergoes adjustments according to our learning needs.

This is what happened to Marlene who, after so many setbacks, found the path that would lead her to progress, reaching the desired goals and planning the future with Paulo José.

That day, the couple was having a snack at a well-known bakery when Paulo José surprised Marlene by talking about marriage.

– What do you think about starting to think about us starting to think about marriage? We have been together for a long time, and I am sure of my feelings, my love.

– We need to mature that idea, dear – said Marlene. First, we need to have our home.

– Yes, you are right! I saw a house very close to your atelier. It's beautiful and... it's for sale! Maybe we can visit it? I have some savings saved up and I think I can afford to buy the house and the furniture.

– I have also been saving some money, but not much, as I have expenses for my daughter. I think that no harm will come to us from visiting this house!

– What do you say we schedule it for next week? I'll talk to the broker.

– I agree, but first, we need to talk to our families – Marlene worried.

– Yes! Let's arrange a dinner party at my house to let everyone know. I'm sure my mother will be very happy with the news and will help us a lot. I am also sure you will fall in love with the house, my love, because it has a beautiful garden, just the way you like it.

– How wonderful! You know my mom and I love flowers. May I ask you a favor? I would very much like Raul to be at this dinner, my love, because he is my daughter's godfather and my best friend. Raul is the brother I never had.

– Of course! I like him very much. Let's invite him. Darling, I'm sure that we'll be very happy! I love you and I will be a great father to Maria Helena, that is, if you allow me, because I already love that little girl as if she were my own daughter and I feel that we have a reciprocal affection.

– She is very attached to you. And I truly feel that you will be the best father in the world.

✳ ✳ ✳

Paulo José called the realtor and made an appointment to visit the property. Soon after lunchtime he arrived at the atelier and Marlene was already waiting for him. They didn't have to drive, because the house was only two blocks away.

Marlene was delighted with the house as soon as she saw it. The property, although in need of some repairs, was located on an excellent street that was well wooded and safe.

The couple, by mutual agreement, decided to make a proposal to the owners. Paulo José would take care of everything, because over the years he had gotten used to the bureaucratic paperwork helping his father in the family business. After five days, he received the long-awaited positive answer.

Not holding back his happiness, Paulo José did not want to waste any time and told his fiancée the news:

– Marlene, I have a surprise for you!

– A good surprise?

– Yes, very good! They accepted our offer. The house is ours!

– My God! What a joy, my love! We're going to have a home!

Euphoric, Marlene called Raul's office to tell her best friend the news.

– Raul, my friend, miss you! How many days since we last saw each other?

– Marlene, I apologize for being at fault with you and my goddaughter. Don't be upset. I'm stuck at work. There are too many tasks.

– I have something new to tell you.

– Speak, I want to know everything! What's new?

– Paulo José and I are getting married, and we have just bought a beautiful house with a garden and everything.

– I don't believe it! Really?

Marlene started laughing at the tone of astonishment in Raul's voice.

Recovering from his fright the boy summoned his friend:

– So let Paulo José know that I will always be a distinguished visitor in this home, huh?!

– Of course! He likes you very much and I am sure he will always welcome you very well.

– I am very happy for you because I know how much you have suffered. I am sure that Paulo José will make you very happy my friend.

– I have another surprise. We are having a dinner party at his parents' house to announce our union and you are invited!

– I'll be there with pleasure! It's an honor to be by your side at this moment. Thank you, my friend. But when will the dinner be?

– We intend to schedule it in a fortnight.

– I will be there for sure. You can count on me.

✱ ✱ ✱

The days that preceded the dinner were days of anticipation for Marlene and Paulo José because the couple was more and more in love each day.

Eunice, the hostess of the house took care of all the details with great care. The lady was really happy for her son and wanted everything to be perfect to welcome the guests. She had personally prepared the menu for the celebration and ordered delicate flowers to adorn the long dining table. With her heart overflowing with joy, Eunice only wished that Paulo José would be truly happy.

Marlene looked especially beautiful that evening. She had chosen a dress with a simple cut but with an excellent fit that highlighted the girl's well-made body. Paulo José never tired of complimenting her, which made her blush with joy.

The starry night was perfect for the celebration of such a special date, and when the meal was served, Paulo José announced the engagement, which was applauded by almost everyone presents except for the groom's father, who was very upset by the news. Nothing, however, could shake the boy's decision, for he was certain of his love for Marlene.

The wedding date was set for four months from now, long enough for the proclamations to take place.

After dinner, Marlene talked to Paulo José about the disappointment she had noticed on her future father-in-law's face.

– Marlene, for me this is nothing new. We have to understand that some people often believe that they are the masters of other people's wills. My father is not the master of my choices. In time he will understand that you are the person I chose to be my wife and the mother of my children.

– I understand. I just didn't want to cause any ill feeling in your family.

– Let it go. Soon, soon my father will accept you. He has no other way.

– You are right. Let's do our best and put our afflictions in the hands of spirituality.

***

The preparations for the wedding began and the bride and groom were overjoyed. After buying the house, Marlene and Paulo José began to furnish it with tasteful furniture, sophisticated curtains and many art objects bought in the most elegant galleries in town. Paulo José made every effort to please his bride.

In the midst of this joyful atmosphere, even though she wished her daughter happiness, Emília became sad every day because she suffered in anticipation of how much she would miss her granddaughter. The lady reflected a lot on the subject and decided to have a conversation with Marlene, who was having her morning meal in the pantry.

– Good morning, Mom!

– Good morning, Marlene! If you don't mind, I would like to talk to you for a while.

Noticing the concern in her mother's face, the girl only nodded positively.

– My daughter, I beg you... leave Maria Helena to me. How will your father and I live without her?

– Mother, I won't keep her from you. We will always be here, and she can spend some weekends with you. I want to have more children soon, and for Maria Helena it will be very good to live with siblings.

– I know, but she may not adapt to the new routine because this is her home. Besides, you have to work, my daughter. How will you organize these matters?

– Mom, my daughter is in love with Paulo José, and he is also very good to her. Maria Helena needs a father and I know he will be one of the best. Let's do this... I can leave her here during the day, and, at night, she will come home. What do you think? That way, you're not completely separated from her.

Conformed Emília nodded:

– I know it won't be easy, but I have to accept it.

✳ ✳ ✳

The days passed quickly and finally; the big day arrived.

From early on, servants were running from one side to the other to make everything to the satisfaction of the bride and groom.

The wedding was held in a small chapel frequented by Marlene's family in an elegant neighborhood of Rio de Janeiro. The bride and groom could not even imagine that there was someone there who had not been invited. It was Júlio, in spirit, who was there to witness the ceremony.

The boy was very moved to see Marlene and his daughter. Unable to contain himself, he let the tears roll down his face as if they could wash away the terrible anguish he felt. At that moment of emotion, Júlio's grandmother, who had disincarnated about fifteen years before, supported him and asked him to accompany her to the astral world, where he would be sheltered in a spiritual colony until he would be able to move on, free to study and work in the erraticity. Júlio, however, was not yet ready to free himself from the chains that he had created around himself. Still confused by the mental disturbance, the boy thanked her but refused her help, telling the grandmother that he deserved all the suffering he was facing because of the great evil he had done in life.

After the party, Marlene and Paulo José traveled to Europe for their honeymoon. The couple stayed away for about fifteen days. During this period, Maria Helena stayed under the care of her grandparents, much to the happiness of Emília, who was very attached to her granddaughter.

The trip was enchanting. Together, Marlene and Paulo José visited museums and churches, walked through the squares of beautiful Italy and enjoyed candlelight dinners in romantic Paris. Every day, the couple discovered more affinities. The girl's eyes shone with pleasure when she contemplated her beloved's face, and they admired each other. Love had made its home in those imperfect hearts that, firm in the purpose of advancing in this earthly journey, worked for their constant improvement.

And so, they returned to a new life together. Marlene resumed her work in the atelier, where she became more and more fulfilled as a professional, and Paulo José went back to work with his father, who saw in his son his right arm.

CHAPTER 17

Little by little, Dionísio got used to his son's marriage, but he still had reservations about his daughter-in-law. Eunice, enchanted with Maria Helena, asked the girl to call her grandma, which was promptly answered by the child.

Maria Helena, in her childish innocence, asked her grandmother if she could also call Dionísio grandpa.

– Honey, I love you very much, and you can call him grandpa... but, if he ever tells you not to call him that, don't be sad, because that is his way.

Little by little, Maria Helena began to get closer to Dionísio. One day, she came to his side and said:

– Grandpa, look at the surprise I brought for you.

Dionísio stood there not knowing how to behave in front of Maria Helena.

– What is the surprise, honey?

Maria Helena showed Dionísio a drawing she had made especially for him. When the girl handed over the paper, the emotion was strong at that moment, and Dionísio hugged her saying:

– Grandpa liked it very much, my granddaughter!

Dionísio began to treat Maria Helena as his true granddaughter and showered the little girl with pampering. And from then on, all the little girl's birthdays were celebrated with a beautiful party.

Paulo José was also very attached to the child and, with Marlene's permission, adopted Maria Helena. From then on, she would officially be his daughter.

The family was united, making plans for the future. Only sometimes a shadow of sadness crossed Marlene's face, because even though she had been married for some time, she still could not get pregnant. Her traumas were very big, but Raul, her friend, always present, gave her a lot of strength so that she would not give up.

Marlene woke up early and in a good mood. She got ready and went down to the pantry for breakfast. By this time, the maid had already arrived to prepare breakfast. Before Marlene entered the pantry, the phone rang, and she answered it on the second ring:

– Daughter, I need you to come here quickly. Your father was very ill early in the morning, but he didn't want to go to the hospital. I don't know what to do – nervous, Emília spat out the words.

– Try to stay calm, mom. I'll be there soon. Just wait. Desperate, Marlene went upstairs to tell her husband the news and ask him to accompany her to her parents' house. Before leaving she left instructions for the maid to take care of Maria Helena.

The way to her parents' house was one of apprehension for Marlene. What had happened to João Alberto? Paulo José spoke words of comfort to his wife as he drove quickly through the city streets.

When they arrived at the Fiorucci family's home, the couple was startled by João Alberto's state of health, who was very pale and could hardly speak. Without further delay, Paulo José and Marlene managed to take him to the hospital.

The doctor who treated João Alberto decided to admit him after analyzing the test results. According to the diagnosis, João Alberto had a severe case of tuberculosis and also complications due to a malfunctioning liver. The patient's condition was serious and required intensive medical care.

In the waiting room, desperation overcame everyone who felt sorry for João Alberto's condition. There was no doubt that the situation was delicate. Time dragged on without the family receiving any encouraging news about the patient, who, after a week of agony, fell into a deep coma and died.

It was a time of deep sorrow for Emília and Marlene, who had lost their mainstay, for João Alberto was a zealous father and a loving husband. During all those years and in many situations, he had kept secret the afflictions that gnawed at his soul so as not to cause the family any trouble.

Despite all the support she received from Raul and Paulo José's family, Marlene, in the days that followed her father's death, was overcome by a deep sadness, however, she sought help of sincere prayer and the lessons learned at the Spiritist Center. Little by little, the girl accepted that only João

Alberto's earthly life had come to an end, but that the spirit is eternal and that, free from the carnal body, he would begin a new journey toward evolution.

At that moment, it was urgent that Marlene support her mother by offering her a shoulder to help her face the pain of separation and the homesickness. So, the girl convinced Emília that the best thing to do would be to spend a few days at her house, in her company, with Paulo José and especially with the sweet Maria Helena, who would brighten her sad days until she recovered.

The stay in her daughter's house did the widow a lot of good, because the residence was surrounded by an aura of harmony and tranquility, possible only in homes that cultivate love and understanding among its residents. After three months, Emília decided to return home and resume her activities. Marlene, in turn, had been talking to Alexandre, a cousin she had a close relationship with, because she would like him to take over the family business. The girl did not want to take over the company since she felt satisfied working in the atelier.

Alexandre was very receptive to the invitation and asked his cousin to give him a period of one month to quit his current job and plan to move to the capital, since he lived in a country town. Once this was done, the boy settled in Rio de Janeiro, and soon started working for the company. Alexandre had a La degree but understood a lot about administration. In this way, he was able to put everything in order much sooner than expected.

Raul was surprised by Alexandre's competence and the two got along very well working together. Carlos decided to step away from the company for a while because he was exhausted and wanted to enjoy life a little. And so, the administration of the company remained in the hands of Raul and Alexandre, and they achieved excellent results in their first year of management, increasing sales.

Little by little, the friendship between the two boys grew stronger, and Raul fell in love with Alexandre without being able to help it, but he was afraid to declaring himself and pushing his friend away.

Alexandre was living temporarily at Emilia's house, to keep her company and one afternoon, the woman, very worried, called Raul and asked him to come to her house, because she needed to talk to someone.

The very solicitous boy promptly answered Marlene's mother's call, and upon arriving at the residence, he was eagerly received by the hostess. After the greetings, Emília introduced the subject without delay.

– Raul, please, I need your help, because I have been dreaming constantly about João Alberto. In the dream, he always says that he needs to tell me something and begs my forgiveness. I don't know how to act. I think I need to go to the center.

– Sure, I will talk to Mrs. Mercedes. Maybe you will get a message from him?

– Talk to her and get back to me. But please don't say anything to Marlene.

– Don't worry, Mrs. Emília. This matter will remain between us.

After the goodbyes, Raul promptly returned to the company. There, he quickly called Mercedes who asked the boy to take Emília to the spiritist center the next night.

✸✸✸

Raul sped up his pace because he was late for his appointment with Emília, who was anxiously waiting for him to go to the Spiritist Center together.

Later, Raul and Emília arrived at the center, a few minutes before the session was to begin and were instructed by Mercedes to put João Alberto's name in the prayer box. Anxiously, the two waited for news of the deceased, but unfortunately, they received nothing.

– Mrs. Emília, don't be discouraged. That's just the way it is. You don't always get a message – said Raul.

– It's okay, I understand. Marlene has already explained some things to me.

Raul and Emília attended weekly sessions at the Spiritist Center in the hope of receiving some news, which only happened after a few weeks.

João Alberto was there accompanied by his father, Manoel, ready to dictate the message his wife was anxiously waiting for.

"Dear Emilia, I am well and content with my departure. My father is here with me. I need to confess something to you. During my earthly passage I had another daughter, whose name is Eloísa,

the result of an extra–marital relationship. Francisca, my daughter's mother, was married to an alcoholic man and worked in the company with me. We ended up getting involved. I was always afraid to reveal the truth to you, because I thought you would not accept it. Today, Eloísa is 22 years old, and I would like very much you to look for her because she needs help. I ask your forgiveness for this secret and for hurting you, but I could not have peace until told you everything."

With love, João Alberto

– Raul, I can't believe that! You must be kidding me. Did you know anything?

– No, Mrs. Emília. And I'm sure even my father didn't know that. I only know who this Francisca is. It's been about three years since she left the company for health reasons.

– My God, how will I tell Marlene about that?

– Try to be strong once more, Mrs. Emília. I will accompany you. Together, we will talk to Marlene, don't worry. As I understand it, we need to do that so that Mr. João Alberto can have peace.

Emília, mourned her pain, not knowing what to think. The woman felt betrayed by her husband, because she never imagined that João Alberto could act in such a vile way. Disconsolate, she asked Raul for some time to reflect.

The boy nodded and accompanied Emília home. Raul knew that the Fiorucci matriarch would need some time to accept the situation and to understand that our actions are only reflections of our knowledge at any given time. Often guided only by our impulses, we hurt those who we hold dear to us without any genuine intention of cause them harm. João Alberto was wrong, but it is never too late to redeem and ask for forgiveness. We are imperfect spirits seeking redemption.

So, after three days, Emília called Raul and asked him to try to locate Francisca, the former employee of the company.

The task was not difficult because the boy had access to the personnel department files. The same day, Emília went to the place indicated by Raul.

In front of Francisca's house, Emília observed that it was a simple but dignified house. The white and blue façade attested to the zeal of the residents whose well-kept garden showed a taste for a variety of flowers.

Resolute, Emília clapped her hands to attract attention inside the house. Soon after, a girl came to answer her.

– Yes! What do you want?

As soon as Emília saw Eloísa, she instantly imagined that it was João Alberto's daughter, because the girl had the same blue eyes as her father.

– I would like to speak with Mrs. Francisca. My name is Emília. I am Mr. João Alberto Fiorucci's wife.

Eloísa became pale and could barely speak.

– At the moment my mother is not here. She went to the doctor.

– Do you think she'll be long?

– No. She should be back by now.

– Okay. I'll wait until she comes back.

– Do you want to come in?

– I won't get in your way? I don't want to bother you.

Through a friend who still worked at the company, Francisca learned of João Alberto's death and passed the news on to her daughter.

After a few minutes, Francisca arrived home and when she opened the door, she was startled to find Emília standing there, in her living room.

– Good afternoon!

– Good afternoon, Francisca! How are you? Excuse me for coming to your house, but I really need to talk to you.

– You are Mrs. Emília, Mr. João Alberto's wife, right?

– Yes, that's right. I believe the lady already knows the reason for my visit.

– Yes, I suspect so. I believe you want to know about your husband and me.

– Look... I don't even know where to start, because I'm still very shocked by what I learned, because my husband and I had a solid marriage. At least that's what I always thought.... I don't think I ever gave him any reason to look for another woman.

– I know...he really loved you very much. All there was between us was just a physical attraction, there was no love.

– Please, Francisca, I don't want to know the intimate details. But answer me: is your daughter really João Alberto's? I would really like you to be honest, because there is no going back, and I am not here to judge anyone. But I need to know the truth.

– So, I am going to tell you the truth. Eloísa is indeed João Alberto's daughter, and he knew it, so much so that he accompanied her growth and helped me to raise her within his means. I never demanded anything from him because I always knew that João Alberto had a family. My husband was an alcoholic, and we had nothing left when I got pregnant. He knew that Eloísa was not his daughter, but he still registered her and always treated her very well and with love. João Alberto and I would meet and spend a few hours together, but I knew it would never go beyond that. As I loved him very much, I submitted myself to that relationship. When my daughter turned 12, I told her the whole truth because João Alberto had always been very loving with her. We always went for walks, even though she didn't know anything about it. He liked to give her presents, and Eloísa believed him to be a friend of mine. However, upon learning the truth, her heart was very divided, because she did not want to hurt her foster father, who had taken her as a daughter. Little by little, however, the two grew closer.

– When I separated from my husband, João Alberto came to see her every day, accompanied her studies, that is, he was a very present and dedicated father.

At that moment, Eloísa came into the room and asked Emilia's forgiveness for everything, hugged her and said:

– I know that the pain is immense...

Francisca lowered her head and began to cry.

– I was too weak. Even though he did not love me, I loved with all my heart. João Alberto always made it very clear that you were the woman he loved.

– I need to digest all that and I still have to tell Marlene the whole story. I also know that you, Eloísa, have rights to the inheritance João Alberto left, but I need some time.

– Mrs. Emília, I don't want anything. That's not fair. Neither you nor your daughter have to give me anything! I suffered a lot when I heard that my father was gone, and I couldn't even say goodbye. I ask God to take care of him and that he is well wherever he is.

– You are entitled, yes, and I know that he wants you to receive what is yours to help your studies and your future. I would very much like Marlene to meet you, because we can't deny that you are sisters.

Emília said goodbye to Eloísa and Francisca and left very shaken by all that she had learned. She still could not believe that her husband had been unfaithful to her.

After two days and after overcoming the initial shock that the news had caused, Emília decided to have a frank talk with Marlene, who, upon hearing her mother's revelations, could not express what she was feeling.

– Mom, this must be some kind of sick joke! Dad? Are you sure about that? I can't believe it.

– Yes, my daughter. Until now I'm stunned by all these revelations. It was very difficult to get all that into my head, but I had to be strong and face the situation. Your sister's name is Eloísa, and her mother's name is Francisca. She was an employee of the company. Daughter, can I make a big request: do not ignore your sister, because this girl is not to blame for anything that has happened.

– Mom, I need some time. How could Dad do that to you? What a disappointment, my God!

Emília, still hurt by her husband's betrayal, tried to calm her daughter.

– You have to be strong, my daughter. There is no point in feeling anger toward your father. We need to understand what happened and handle the situation in the best way we can.

– How can I not feel anger and indignation? Why did he do that to you, who have always been an exemplary wife? Mom, you always took care of him with dedication and love!

– My daughter, take the time to reflect on everything I have told you. You are very intelligent and enlightened. I know you will do your best.

The two women said goodbye, and Marlene made her way to her residence.

When Marlene arrived home, Marlene found her husband and told him all that had happened. Paulo José was very surprised with the story and did not know what to say to his wife, because he did not want to make a hasty judgment about his father–in–law's actions. He then hugged his wife, and the two remained entwined for several moments.

The girl calmed down little by little and asked her husband to leave her alone, because she needed to think more about the decision she had to make. Resolute, Marlene picked up the phone and called Raul.

After the initial greetings, Marlene was direct:

– Raul, I need to talk to you!

– Okay. Do you want me to come to your house?

– No, Raul. Let's meet at that tearoom near your apartment.

– Okay, I'll be there at 3:00 pm. Is that okay?

– Great. See you there!

✳ ✳ ✳

Marlene arrived on the scene minutes after Raul, who was very anxious to know what was going on.

– Hello, Raul! Sorry to bother you, but you're the only person I trust to deal with this issue.

– Wow, I'm curious to know what's going on.

– I am very bad. I found out something about my father... still very hard to believe.

– Tell me soon, my dear! You know I am there for you.

– Raul, my father had another daughter, who was the result of an extramarital relationship with a woman who was an employee of the company. I can't believe it, much less accept it. It's absurd that my mother has to live with that betrayal! My father always showed himself to be such a correct man, so upright! In all my life, that would be the last thing I thought my father would do.

– Marlene, I know all of this is very painful, even more so now that he is gone. It's a lot of pain together, but you need to accept it. There is no other way. Besides, this girl is not to blame for what happened to her the parents' mistakes. Have you ever thought that she is as much a victim of that situation as you are? Try to understand, because maybe your mother will suffer less.

Marlene was thoughtful, because she knew that she needed to put her indignation aside and act justly. She also knew that Emília was a just and loyal woman and would give Eloísa everything she that was rightfully hers.

The two continued talking and Raul tried to distract Marlene's mind with more pleasant subjects.

At home, Emília thought it best to give her daughter a few days to better analyze the situation, but she would not let it go any longer than necessary. It was imperative that they talk to Francisca and Eloísa about João Alberto's inheritance.

Emília was sure that the events of the last few days were the fruit of divine providence, acting for her to turn her life around, because after her widowhood she had been very bitter, without knowing what direction to take. The Fiorucci matriarch dedicated her life to taking care of the house, her husband, her daughter and more recently her granddaughter, but had never done anything for herself. So, she decided to "shake off the dust" and take charge of her own life. Emília had always wanted to study pharmacy and work in an apothecary shop, but João Alberto had never allowed her to do so. Then she decided to talk to Marlene, because she was sure that her daughter would support her in the achieving her dreams.

A few days later, while they were talking, Emília shared her plans with her daughter.

– Wow, Mom, how wonderful! Yes, you should open an apothecary shop! It will renew your life. You have always been so submissive, but now it's your turn to be happy. And be sure that I'll help you achieve all of that.

– Ah, daughter, I count on your help! I need more joy in my life, a purpose. And I ask you, Marlene, do not to reject Eloísa. She is your sister, and she reminds me a lot of you.

– Mom, I have talked a lot to Raul, and he has helped me to understand some things better. Little by little, he is opening my heart, making me see the situation from another angle. My dear friend has a sneaky way of telling the truths I need to hear.

After a pause, she continued:

– Mom, invite Mrs. Francisca over for tea so I can get to know them.

– My daughter, what a joy! I knew you would do that. You are good at heart and very generous. You just needed some time to think.

Emília then made the invitation to Francisca and Eloísa, who promptly accepted.

On the appointed date, Marlene woke up very anxious to meet Eloísa, wondering how that meeting would go. Would she really accept her or reject her at the last moment?

Upon seeing her sister Marlene was deeply moved. She did not expect to have that reaction, but the resemblance between them was undeniable. Eloísa, very ashamed, looked at Marlene and asked her forgiveness. The moment was of singularly moving. After the sisters exchanged a tight hug, everyone in the room was moved. Tears were the companions of those four women, who were united by the wisdom of life, even though circumstances caused them so much pain.

Emília, then, asked Francisca once again to accept her help because she knew that she and Eloísa were having difficulties, but the woman did not want to be a burden to her ex-lover's wife and declined the offer, saying that she wanted to work for her own livelihood. Eloísa also helped her mother a lot, who made sweets to sell, but life had become even more difficult after João Alberto's death.

Supported by spiritual friends, the four women began a close friendship there. Later, Eloísa met María Helena and fell in love with her niece. The atmosphere in the house was one of peace and harmony. There, forgiveness took up residence and a new cycle began.

✳ ✳ ✳

One day, Raul had an idea while talking to Marlene:

– Honey, we could put Eloísa to work in the company. I think this might be a good solution for everyone.

– Wow, Raul, what a great idea! My sister really needs help. What do you say we go to her house and personally extend the invitation?

Promptly, the two friends went to Francisca's house and were welcomed with genuine joy by the residents.

Eloísa was very happy with the proposal and accepted the invitation immediately, but Francisca was very worried, because she was afraid that her daughter would be embarrassed, after all, people would soon know that the girl was João Alberto's daughter because of her resemblance to Marlene.

– Mrs. Francisca, don't worry. I am in the company every day and I will help your daughter. I will be there to protect her.

– Thank you, Raul. You are really a very special person, and I trust you, but if there is any trouble, I would rather Eloísa just walk away right away.

– Calm down, mom! This is an excellent opportunity that my sister and Raul are offering me. I can't let it go. But, Raul, what will I do there?

– You'll learn a little bit about everything to know how the company works, and then we'll see.

– Great! When can I start? I need to prepare myself.

– Three days from now. Is that okay?

– It is a deal! I'll be there.

Three days after that conversation, Eloísa started working at the company. She was a diligent girl, very polite and very willing to learn.

Involved in her duties, Eloísa was not even aware that time had passed quickly. She had been working in her father's company for a year. Eloísa and Francisca had moved away from house, because Marlene, as part of her inheritance, had given her sister a property near the company.

Eloísa was reconciling her work with her studies, because she wanted to be better prepared to help Raúl in the administration of the company.

The family ties also grew closer every day. Maria Helena loved to visit Eloísa, and Francisca, to please the child, always baked the cakes that she loved so much. Besides, whenever Marlene needed help, Francisca was always ready to help to take care of Maria Helena, a task that the lovely lady performed with much love and care.

CHAPTER 18

One afternoon, Marlene was exhausted and feeling very ill. Paulo José was worried about his wife's health and asked her to go to see a doctor, because the girl was very upset, which was not normal for her. Suspicious, Marlene made an appointment with the doctor she trusted, because her rules were late.

When she arrived at the doctor's office, Marlene was seen by the doctor, who was concerned about the patient's pallor and asked her to do some routine tests and, of course, a pregnancy test, since the girl had reported her menstrual delay.

– Doctor, am I pregnant?

– I don't know, Marlene. I ask you to go to a laboratory you trust, run the tests and bring me the results as soon as possible.

– Doctor, I feel so weak... Sometimes I don't even feel like getting up.

– Calm down, I will help you. Be patient.

Marlene had the tests done but preferred to wait for the results before sharing her suspicions with her husband.

After ten days the suspicions were confirmed. To Marlene's dismay, she was pregnant. It was as if a movie played in her mind again, bringing all the fear of her past back.

When she got home, Marlene had a hard time telling Paulo José the news.

– Marlene, what did your tests show, my love? I'm very worried!

She began to tremble involuntarily, and her expression was of panic.

– My love, what happened? Is it that bad? Tell me!

– Paulo José, I have something to tell you... but I don't know how you will take this news. I am pregnant!

Paulo José stood still for a moment, looking into his wife's eyes, and then he embraced her with emotion. Tears were rolled from his eyes and wet his face.

– My love, you made me the happiest man in the world! I need to tell my family. Let's arrange a dinner here at home to tell everyone the news!

Paulo José's reaction to the news made a huge weight off Marlene's back.

– Of course, my love. Can I call my mother, Raul and my sister?

– O course! Call whoever you want!

Paulo José was very happy with the news that he would be a father.

On the date set for the dinner, the guests were received with great care by the host couple.

After the meal, which was highly praised by all present, Paulo José announced Marlene's pregnancy, and everyone was thrilled and congratulated the couple. Dionísio was very move because he had been slow to accept his daughter–in–law, but now he was very grateful to her.

– You are an excellent wife and mother, Marlene. My son is very lucky to have married you.

Marlene was overjoyed to be a mother, but her health required care. The doctor had recommended that she rest because she was suffering from acute anemia.

Paulo José did not know what to do to please Marlene during her pregnancy. By this time, Maria Helena was already calling him father, which the boy's heart very happy.

Unfortunately, the joy of pregnancy did not stop Marlene from falling into depression. Although Eloísa and Raul helped her a lot, she could not find the strength to react.

Always supported by his family, Paulo José became desperate as he watched his wife wither away daily and get worse every day. The doctor accompanying her pregnancy tried to calm the girl's family, saying that, if Marlene kept her pregnancy, the child would be born normal. The girl's family and friends, however, feared for the baby's life and for Marlene herself, who was losing weight and would not get out of bed.

Raul, then, decided to go to the Mercedes' center to ask for help for his friend. In that peaceful and harmonious environment, the group, assisted by charitable brothers, sent many vibrations to the sick girl and, little by little, she began to respond. Mercedes also made some visits to Marlene and gave her restorative passes.

Time moved slowly for those in distress, and Marlene reached her fifth month of pregnancy. One night, she had a dream with Júlio, in which he once again, asked her forgiveness. The boy also asked her to take Maria Helena to meet his family.

At dawn, Marlene woke up with the memory of the dream, but she did not think much about it because she did not want to touch the past. Although she chose not to pay any attention to the subject, she spent the day worn out because she had lost a lot of energy during the night's encounter.

After a few days, Marlene, already tired of staying at home, asked Paulo José to take her to the atelier, because she would like to resume her activities, even though slowly. Concerned with his wife's health and with the fact that Marlene was a high-risk pregnancy he asked her to wait a little longer. The girl, however, insisted and he eventually gave in to her wishes.

When they arrived at the atelier, Lourdes was very happy to see the partner back.

– Lourdes, my friend, I would like to resume my activities little by little to help you, because I know you are very busy. My absence from work has worried me a lot.

– I am happy, darling, but your health and the baby's health come first, so take it easy.

– I will come in the morning and help you with the administration.

The atelier was doing very well and there was no lack of clients. Lourdes continued to be responsible for the creation of the pieces and Marlene, who managed the company, was very attentive to everyone. Two more girls had been hired to make the pieces, and the atelier prospered each day.

Emília decided to go to the atelier to see how her daughter was doing.

– Are you back yet?

– Yes, mom, I am. I need to occupy my mind.

– You're right. And I feel that I also need to occupy my mind. I have decided that I will open my own apothecary shop. As soon as I find a place and set up the structure, I will hire a pharmacist in charge for the place.

– I am very happy for you, Mom. Let's talk to Raul! I am sure he will be able to help find the ideal professional.

The next day, Marlene and Emília went to Raul, who offered to help them with whatever was necessary. After a few days of searching, they found a great commercial point that was in a well-known avenue in Rio de Janeiro. Although the rent was a little high, Emília, enthusiastically, closed the deal and began to set up the apothecary.

The Fiorucci matriarch hired a pharmacist indicated by a family friend. Hélio had been away from work for a long time because his wife had faced a terrible illness and unfortunately passed away.

As soon as it was ready, Emília's long-awaited apothecary was inaugurated in a festive atmosphere, after all, the Fiorucci matriarch was finally following an old dream – something that gave meaning to her life.

Every day, Emília showed up for work and her desire to learn was contagious. The only thing that bothered her was the distance of her residence to the apothecary, so she decided to put her property up for sale and move. Eventually, Emília rented a house very close to her work and began to have more time for herself.

Dedicated to his work, Hélio helped Emília a lot and talked to her about how lonely he felt because his wife had left. Besides, they had not had any children, which made his life even lonelier. Their daily life now consisted of working and the apothecary's shop.

The friendship between them grew every day. With the excuse of keeping each other company, Hélio began to invite Emília to go for walks. One day, they would go to the square, the next day, to the park. They also frequented the local coffee shops. For Emília, the pleasure of going to a coffee shop was indescribable, because she loved to taste delicious coffee accompanied by sweets treats.

Marlene began to notice that her mother was very different, happier and more at ease with life. Bluntly, the girl then asked Emília if she had any feelings for Hélio.

– Of course not, Marlene! He is just a good friend.

– Mom, you have every right to rebuild your life. Besides having suffered immensely from Dad's betrayal, you need to understand that he's gone. Nothing is stopping you from meeting someone and falling in love again.

Emília, then, started to smile before replying:

– But Mr. Hélio only sees me as a good friend!

– I don't see it that way, Mom. To me, he likes you. Have you noticed that Mr. Hélio is always by your side? Notice that, even on his days off, he doesn't want to stay away from you! If he declares himself, give happiness a chance!

– I don't know, daughter. I think my time has already passed, Marlene. I'm too old. Your father was my only man.

– Mom, I insist: Dad is no longer here, and loneliness is very bad. No one grows old for love, Mom. No one. As long as there's life in our body there's room for love to blossom.

– That's okay, my daughter. I'll think more about that.

Marlene really wanted her mother to give love a chance, because she wanted Emília to be happy.

Without further ado, she went to Emília's suitor.

– How are you, Mr. Hélio?

– Hello, Marlene. I am very well. And you? Are you looking forward to the arrival of the child?

– Yes, I am! The pregnancy still demands care, but I'm very happy. Paulo José is also very excited to increase the family!

– Ah, what a joy! Unfortunately, I didn't have children. I'm very sorry about that.

Mr. Hélio... Have you ever thought about having a relationship with a woman again? Getting married again?

The man was taken by surprise by Marlene's question, but he did not hesitate to answer.

– I will not lie to you, Marlene. I've often thought many times about having a new wife. Living alone, without someone to share the days with is hard.

– Then, why don't you marry my mother?!

Emília, who was just entering the room, turned pale at Marlene's joke.

– My daughter, what is that? You are leaving Mr. Hélio speechless.

Smiling, Marlene asked:

– What's the problem, Mom? You are both widowed and alone, I'd love that union to come true!

A little tense, Hélio began to laugh, but deep inside that was what he wanted. Even at 65, Emília was still a beautiful woman. Hélio was younger than her, he was 60, but it was as if that difference did not exist.

After this amusing episode, Hélio gradually came around until he decided to propose to Emília. Still stuck in the past, she was nevertheless very afraid.

– You're not doing this to please my daughter, are you?

– I would never do that! I hold you in high esteem, Mrs. Emília. I am a free and unimpeded man, and I would like to rebuild my life with you, because you are a beautiful and generous woman who has also enchanted my heart. I know I can make you very happy. Give me this opportunity.

– I think we can try, but we are together all the time Hélio... We can't confuse our work with dating.

– Yes, Mrs. Emília, you're right. So, let's try it!

– Just call me Emília, please.

A kiss sealed that special moment between two souls who, with so many affinities, sought the joy of a life together.

From that day on, the couple began their courtship. During this period, Hélio was a great help to Emília, who could not count on her daughter, who was still facing the challenges of a risky pregnancy. Little by little, Hélio became a father to Marlene and a grandfather to Maria Helena.

✸ ✸ ✸

Marlene was approaching the ninth month of pregnancy and had to be put on absolute bed rest. One morning, she began to feel the first contractions and was taken to the hospital. The girl's condition was not good. Marlene's blood pressure was high, which worried the doctors. The pregnant woman had terrible drowsiness and saw Júlio's spirit besides her who said:

– I am here to protect you. You will give birth to a girl, who is the incarnation of your grandmother Irca.

During labor, Marlene heard many voices and saw many people around her who seemed to be helping her. The girl had the impression that the room was full of people and that people were asking her to calm down.

Júlio was standing next to Marlene, which was very strange to her. Then, she felt a very strong pain and started screaming for help. At that moment they took her to the delivery room and, in a short time, Marlene and Paulo José's daughter was born, a big and healthy girl.

Due to the strain of labor, Marlene became very weak and had some bleeding, which caused to be hospitalized for a few more days than expected.

Moved by the sight of his daughter, Paulo José named her Ester. With the little girl in his arms, he said a heartfelt prayer, thanking God for having watched over the life of his daughter and his wife. As he nursed the baby, Paulo José thought about all the events that would take place that day. Marlene's involvement in the past, the reunion with the girl, the happy marriage. He kissed his daughter's forehead and finally concluded that everything in life was right, no matter what happened.

* * *

When she was discharged, Marlene went home where Emília and Eunice helped her with Ester's care. Although still a little weak, the girl was happy to have the little girl in her arms and surrounded by her family.

A few days after the birth, something very strange began to happen to Marlene. The girl began to have constant visions, and, in several dreams, she found herself with Júlio.

Marlene took the opportunity to read a book, because she always enjoyed reading. Suddenly, however, she got up and went to Ester's crib to see if her daughter was asleep. When she entered the room, she saw a sphere of white light approaching her daughter's crib. Frightened, Marlene took her daughter in her arms and ran to call Mercedes.

During the phone conversation, she told what she had seen:

– My daughter, you are very sensitive and have a lot of mediumships.

– I'm worried about this story of taking Maria Helena to meet Júlio's parents because I don't want to get close to them.

– If you don't want to, that's fine. Leave things as they are because time will take care of all this. Take it easy.

– Will Júlio hurt us, Mrs. Mercedes?

– No, because he is already being helped by a light team. Besides, providing this meeting is only his wish. Take it easy.

After this conversation Marlene became calmer because she trusted Mercedes a lot.

With each passing day Ester showed a rare beauty and won the hearts of her grandparents. Maria Helena, very intelligent, was interested in everything.

✶✶✶

Renata, a good friend of Marlene's, was going through a period of many doubts, because she wanted to live outside of Brazil. Marcos, however, did not accept her plans. They were still dating, and Marcos wanted to get married. She did not feel ready for marriage. During a conversation, she decided to talk to Marlene.

– Renata, you have been together for so long.... I know you love him, think about it. Who knows, maybe in the future you will move out together? I know how you are but at this moment it's not good to make a hasty decision. Try to calm down.

– I think you are right. I know that sometimes I get anxious. Of course, I love Marcos. He is careful with me and has always respected me. I think I need to go to the center to take some passes to calm down.

– I can accompany you because I believe that would also be very good at this time. There are many disturbed spirits that can get in the way of our lives. By taking a pass, we can create new and improve energies, as well as keep ourselves always vigilant and develop the habit of prayer, which connects us to God and to the spirits of light. Marlene always believed in spirituality very much and was sure that the energy received through the pass was very beneficial to all.

The friends continued to exchange confidences and Marlene got to know a little more about her friend's boyfriend.

Marcos was a man with a lot of mediumships and had Ernesto now as one of his mentors. When he was incarnated the spirit of light was a very kind man. In life he did not marry and was the third child of Italian immigrant parents. In time his parents became owners of land used to grow grapes. When they passed away, the boy, even though he had a law degree, took over the land, and his brothers Ângelo and Pedro moved to the city and visited him not frequently. Ernesto always helped the poor a lot and loved animals. He passed away at the age of 43.

One day Marcos took his mother, who had a serious problem with her legs and severe pains, which made it very difficult for her to walk, to a session at the Spiritist Center. When Ernesto saw him, he felt that he already knew the boy from somewhere, and he was right, because in other lives Marcos had been Ernesto's son. The sensation experienced by the spirit was very strong and he began to get closer to Marcos until he became his mentor, according to the designs of spirituality.

As soon as he began to see Ernesto Marcos was frightened, but little by little the spirit showed him that he was good, and there began a friendship between them. Whenever he could, Ernesto helped the boy in his work.

Marcos was very reserved about this subject and feared being called crazy if anyone knew of his mediumistic ability.

A few days later Renata decided to talk to her parents about her wedding, because the renovation of the house that Marcos had bought had finally been completed. After the conversation she had with her friend, the girl opted to postpone her plans to live abroad and go ahead with her plans to marry the boy who was well liked by the bride's family. So, there were no problem to start the preparations for the big party.

Dionísio, who by this time was already a little tired, decided to sell the farm, for Paulo José had long since decided to stay in the city with his wife. The transaction for the sale of the property went smoothly and in six months the farm already belonged to the new owners. Dionísio then decided to give his son a bigger house, since the family had grown.

Happy Paulo José went running to tell Marlene the news, but she did not like the idea of moving, because she liked her house very much.

– Marlene, I think it would be very good for us to live in a bigger house! The children would have more space and since I know you like to garden; I will look for one that has a beautiful space for you to take care of.

– I don't want to bring trouble to you because of that but I prefer it to be in the vicinity of our current residence as I'm already used to the neighborhood.

– You bet! I'll find something that will delight your eyes at first sight. Don't worry, you will be surprised at our new home.

Paulo José continued to be his father's right–hand man in the administration of the business, and Dionísio had recently been gradually stepping away from the company, because he wanted his son to gain confidence so that he could manage everything on his own.

After a few visits and many days of searching Paulo José managed to find a beautiful, terraced house with a garden full of roses that Marlene would love. He promptly closed the deal and soon the whole family moved.

In the back of the house there was an avocado tree and a swing that Maria Helena loved. With time, everyone got used to the new home full of love and affection from its residents.

As a result of the difficult situations, she had faced in the past, Marlene was overly demanding and afraid of making mistakes with her family, which left her with no peace and caused her intense physical exhaustion.

During a conversation Paulo José asked her to seek treatment, which was very difficult for Marlene to understand. Finally, she decided to seek help because she knew she was not well.

Dr. Amadeu, a psychiatrist, was highly recommended by a friend of the girl. After a few consultations, the experienced professional diagnosed that Marlene was suffering from depression and decided to start treatment immediately so that the situation would not worsen. After about twenty days Marlene began to feel some improvement, in part encouraged by the love she had for her children and also by the satisfaction she felt working in the atelier. Gradually the woman resumed her daily activities.

The partners started to have new ideas for the business and decided to open a children's clothing store. They chose as the ideal spot for the new business the center of town, more specifically on Direita street. After some research, they found a wonderful place and set up their business, which would be the first children's clothing store whose chosen name was Lelekas. The public was formed by people of medium to high financial standards and the enterprise was a success. In a few years they had to open four more stores.

Meanwhile, Marlene's daughters were growing every day. Maria Helena was very studious and kind to everyone, and Ester, more independent, liked to do everything by herself, which demanded special care from the mother, who needed to be attentive to the girl. Even though she had so many tasks in raising her daughters, Marlene visited her stores daily to follow closely the development of the business.

One day the businesswoman noticed that in front of one of her stores a girl with a baby in her arms was asking for help. Decided, Marlene approached her:

– Good morning! How are you? I always see you here with your baby.

– Yes, I stay here to ask for help because I've been living on the street since I became pregnant with Carlos. He is the result of a passing relationship and the father disappeared. I was working in a residence as a maid, but they didn't accept me when they found out I was pregnant and sent me away. I will be honest with you... I was not ready to be a mother and I would love to put Carlos in a shelter or give him to someone to raise him so that I could continue my life.

At that moment Marlene looked into the baby's eyes and was heartbroken, but she quickly said goodbye to the woman and returned to the store, where she began to cry. The girl felt a deep sadness for the child's situation but tried to put those thoughts out of her mind, for there must have been some reason why life had placed that mother and child together.

At night, during dinner at their home, Marlene could not contain herself and told Paulo José about what had happened, concluding that she could not forget the baby's eyes. He, however, did not take his wife's story into consideration, merely consoling her with empty words.

After fifteen days Marlene did not see the girl with the baby outside her store again and forgot about it, but one day she decided to go to a market near her house to buy fresh fruit and vegetables and suddenly heard a voice behind her asking for help. When she turned around, she saw that it was Carlos' mother.

– Good afternoon. Is that you? What is your name? Why did you leave the front of the store? I bought some things for the baby, but I couldn't find you anymore.

– My name is Neuza. We were no longer getting help there. I managed to get into a house nearby that is abandoned. It is a very old house, and we are occupying just one room. We share the rest of the property with other families, but it is very difficult to stay there with Carlos.

– Are you still thinking of putting him up for adoption? Are you sure you don't want to keep your son?

– Yes. I know that I'm not a good mother, ma'am. I don't like children and I can't raise him alone.

– Where is the house you are living in?

Neuza then gave the address and explained where it was.

When she got home Marlene talked to Paulo José about the idea of adopting Carlos because after some complications in her last delivery, she ran the risk of not being able to get pregnant again.

– Marlene, this is very serious. What if later this woman wants her child back?

– We can check with your father and do everything right as the law requires. If she repents and wants the child back, she has no further rights to the child.

Marlene and Paulo José decided to talk to Dionísio, who showed them all the paths to adoption. During the weekend Marlene managed to convince her husband to meet the baby and on Saturday afternoon they decided to go to the address Neuza had given them. When they got there, they clapped their hands and Neuza soon appeared at the gate.

– Hello Neuza, good afternoon! This is Paulo José, my husband. We would like to see Carlos. Do you allow us?

– Of course. Come on in.

They entered the abandoned house where Neuza was living with the child and some other families who found in that place a shelter to escape from the violence of the streets and the bad weather.

When they finally arrived at a small corner of the house where Carlos was sleeping on a pile of rags, Marlene, who could not stand the anxiety, did not even wait for her husband's reaction and started asking Neuza:

– Would you give us your son for adoption? We would like to raise Carlos.

Without reaction Paulo José looked startled at Marlene.

– Of course! said Neuza without hesitation. I want my freedom back and to get on with my life and he gets in my way a lot.

Touched by the emotion that he saw in his wife's eyes, Paulo José decided that the best thing to do was to adopt that child. The couple then took Carlos home that same day and since the baby was very malnourished, Marlene gave him a quick bath and took him to her daughters' pediatrician.

Soon after, Carlinhos was already loved by the family. Without many difficulties, the couple, helped by Dionísio, soon managed to complete the adoption of the child. The little boy looked like an angel. He had curly and blond hair and blue eyes. Marlene was delighted with her son of the heart.

Paulo José's parents went to visit their grandchildren almost every day, and Dionísio said that Carlitos reminded him a lot of his brother Toninho, who had died at the age of two. They loved their granddaughters very much, but Carlinhos had conquered his grandfather's heart for good, and he did everything for him.

The child was very smart, happy, and never stopped still. Maria Helena loved her brother, but Ester was a little jealous and fought with him for the attention of their mother, who was very good at teaching them to love each other.

Peace reigned in that blessed home.

On a cold night, however, Carlinhos began to have a fever, cough and tiredness. As soon as morning came, Marlene took the child to the hospital where they diagnosed bronchitis. Thus, the next two years were very difficult.

One day, Marlene was at the salon and a woman overheard her talking about Carlinhos' health problem. The woman was helpful and told her about a witchdoctor who had cured her son of the same problem. Marlene promptly wrote down the address and took her son there.

Catarina – as the witchdoctor was called – prayed for Carlinhos and asked Marlene to return twice to continue the child's spiritual treatment.

Always with great faith, Marlene did everything that was asked of her and little by little Carlinhos was cured of the severe bronchitis that afflicted him. The most intriguing thing was that bronchitis was a recurrent disease in Paulo Jose's family.

When Carlinhos turned five years of age, Marlene explained to the little boy that she was his heart mother. In her home there was a lot of love but there were also many rules that everyone had to follow without distinction. Despite her job in the apothecary's shop, Emília was always present in her grandchildren's lives and helped Marlene to educate them.

As each day passed, love prevailed in Marlene's home, but Ester showed more and more that she was jealous of Carlinhos.

– Paulo José, we treat everyone here the same way. I pay attention to everyone.

– Marlene, I don't think you realize it, but your bond with Carlinhos is very strong.

– Maybe you get that impression because he needs me so much. Still, I will pay more attention to that. I notice that Maria Helena is more attached to you...

– Try to pay a more attention to Ester so that we can confirm if it is really that and cure her nervousness. I've noticed that anything makes her cry and that's not normal.

– But even your parents are attached to Carlinhos, Paulo.

– I know, but we can give Ester a little more care. That's all.

– I will. You're right. I'll do my best to make sure Ester is well.

Although she wanted to, Marlene could not change her attitudes much. It was as if a magnet was always pulled her closer to Carlinhos. Whenever she left for work, she had to leave something of hers close to the boy because he was so attached to her that he was afraid of losing her. The bond was so strong between them that they seemed to be mother and son by blood.

With their stores prospering each day, Marlene and her partner decided to hire a manager to take care of their stores so they would have more time to dedicate to new creations. Lourdes was dating a boy and already thinking about marriage, so a manager to manage the stores would be important for her to take that next step in life.

Marlene commented on the need to hire a manager for the store with her mother–in–law and with Renata, who soon said:

– I have a very competent friend who has just left her old job and is looking for a new position. If you would like, I could introduce her to you.

– Please. Bring her here so that Lourdes and I can meet her.

Renata talked to her friend Solange who agreed to meet the partners at the atelier.

Marlene and Lourdes liked Solange very much and hired her immediately, feeling relieved to share the tasks with one more person.

Solange was single and lived with her mother. She was an excellent daughter. Her brother had passed away two years ago from hepatitis, and Solange's mother had become very ill. Her father had passed away twenty years earlier, and the family's financial life had become difficult. The job brought them great joy because it gave them hope for a better life. Marlene and Lourdes offered Solange a good salary because according to them: "When the employee earns well, the return is even better".

Solange managed the stores very well and even helped to decrease the operating costs. She soon gained the respect of all the employees and her life was divided between her work and her mother. The girl was Marlene and Lourdes' right hand.

Marlene was in charge of the shopping and strived to bring in new products. The stores continued to grow. Paulo José, in turn, was worried because he knew that Marlene was a great businesswoman and that she never stopped, always striving to create something new.

– Marlene, this way you will end up sick. You need to calm down, take a break.

– All right, I will stop. I just need to do a few more things – and, obviously Marlene continued.

CHAPTER 19

With her financial life prospering Marlene decided to buy rental properties. Raul took advantage of the opportunity and rented one of these friend's properties because some time ago he had started to make some changes in his life. He was in a new relationship but had not yet come out. The boy, however, was eager to find the courage to tell everyone. Marlene always supported her friend because she knew how much he had suffered in his last relationship. Raul was a stronghold to help others, but his weakness was love.

A few years ago, on a trip to Spain, Raul met a fortune-teller like those who hang around the streets, who told him that he would have a relationship with a man who had already formed a family. However, time would bring the two together. That man was married and had two children.

At the time Raul did not give much importance to the fortune-teller's words, for he had never wanted to be the pivot of a separation, much less get involved with a married man. This meeting, however, happened as the woman had predicted.

Arthur worked in a company near Raul's, and both had lunch at the same place. From then on, a beautiful friendship began between them and despite the insecurity he felt, Arthur ended up creating in his head a future with Raul because his marriage was going from bad to worse.

The friendship between the two evolved into a relationship. Arthur got to know another side of himself that he had never known before because he had always had many sexual problems with his wife. He did not, however, have the courage to see the truth.

As Arthur became more and more involved with Raul and fell even more in love with the boy, his marriage to Anita became increasingly untenable. He then decided to divorce his wife but without leaving the children destitute. Anita was a very beautiful woman, but Arthur's heart belonged to Raul.

Anita believed that her husband had another woman and not another man. This idea had never crossed her mind. Arthur and Raul assumed the relationship only to a few close friends.

Arthur was very sympathetic to spiritualism, but he had only been twice to a spiritual center because Anita did not like anything to do with spirits. She was Catholic so he used to go to mass with her. Raul decided to take him to the Mercedes' center since Arthur had lost his parents in a short period of time.

Tadeu, Arthur's father, passed away at the age of 79 due to a massive heart attack, and his mother Amélia had passed away at the age of 74 on an operating table.

The couple went to the center on a day when the mediums were preparing to receive messages and Arthur informed the name of his parents. At the end of the session, Tadeu, the boy's father, left him a message apologizing to him because, at the time of his disincarnation, he was very distant from his son. Tadeu was a very hard man with his family and often beat his wife, which caused a fight between him and Arthur ten days before his death. This fight had left the boy shaken at the time. He knew that he was defending his mother but had many feelings for his father. Tadeu then decided, with the help of the Spirituality, to ask his son for forgiveness, saying that Amélia had already forgiven him and was there by his side.

Arthur began to cry non-stop and Raul then, supported his companion and said:

– Forgive your father. It's been a long time. We all make mistakes at some point, and he has seen the error.

Arthur could only nod his head in agreement, and Raul continued:

– But forgive your father from the heart, not just out of mouth. I know how difficult the whole situation must have been. The ignorance of a man is the downfall of a family.

– Since I was a boy, I was very afraid of my father, Raul. My mom was constantly disrespected at home. He would yell and break things. Everything was always very difficult.

– Did he drink or have an addiction?

– No, he had no addiction. He was just a very mean and unbalanced man. He even attacked the animals inside the house. He only stopped these aggressions when we grew up. My mother had to wash clothes to buy what we needed. Because of him we didn't even go to school. I was always the son who faced him the most. I can't have love for him. It is as if I have blocked all of that inside me. Actually, I was really hoping to talk to my mother because I miss her so much. Raul, I will be honest and tell you from the heart.... I really want to forgive but sometimes it is very difficult.

– Pray for your father Arthur so that his spirit will have peace. Today he can see the mistakes he has made, and he will certainly have to make amends at some point in the spirit world. Today you have the opportunity to be here. Forgiveness is evolution. At least do this for yourself and then you will have peace.

– Our life is really fleeting and only here do we create opportunities to fix everything. I, for example, know that I am wrong in not telling my parents about our relationship, but I know how much this can hurt them.... For the love I feel for them I prefer to keep quiet.

Arthur, we have a lot to learn with each other and we need to talk about everything always. I understand your position and I want to be at your side for whatever you need.

In time I intend to talk to my children about us. Now, however, I believe it's too early for that. I have never loved anyone as much as I love you, but I am still not sure about talking to the children about our relationship.

Raul then began to cry with emotion and the two of them looked at each other as if there was no one else there. Raul had already had moments of great sadness in his life, but now his happiness was complete. Although Arthur was still going through a process of divorce, the two were already building a life and a solid relationship together. Contrary to what he had imagined, Raul did not feel guilty because everything had happened naturally. His partner's marriage was already at an end. Raul was not the pivot of the separation.

Marlene went to the center with Raul and Arthur and admired their love. She felt the need to always go there to take passes and pray for her family. Many times, she used to feel the presence of her mentors. Every Tuesday, the three of them would do the gospel at Marlene's house and with time, Paulo José also began to participate in the sessions.

On day of prayer Marlene began to tremble and cry. Raul and Arthur then began to pray for that spirit to communicate, and little by little she began to passive. It was Marcelina, Raul's grandmother, who had been disincarnated nine years ago and was crying because she was so excited to be able to talk to her grandson. The old woman said that she had always known of the grandson's preference for men and that he should not be ashamed of the love he felt for Arthur. Furthermore, Marcelina advised him to at least tell his mother about the relationship, because she would understand. Finally, the elderly woman sent hugs to everyone and said that she was doing very well.

As soon as Marcelina left, Marlene's mentor introduced himself as Brother Cândido de Sa'. From then on, she began to have many visions.

– Marlene, why don't you go to work at the center? – said Raul.

– I guess I'm not ready yet. Let's do the sessions right here at home. My mediumship is surfacing, and I want everything to happen at the right time. I wish that Carlinhos were a little bigger, because he still depends a lot on me. Every time I come home, he won't let go of me, and no matter how much Paulo José gives him attention, my son just wants me, and I can't stop taking care of him. He says that everything I do is better, and he sleeps every night on my lap. Paulo José gets angry, but I know that this is his need. When Carlinhos grows up, that will stop. You know, Raul, my love for him is so great that I can't even imagine that one day my son will grow up and take over his life.

– Carlinhos has won our hearts, Marlene. Your father-in-law can't even hide his preference for him.

– I know. There are connections that come from many lifetimes. Maybe this is the case with them. We have no idea about the invisible ties that bind people together.

※ ※ ※

Time was moving fast and bringing new events. Maria Helena's birthday arrived, and Marlene decided to organize a party at Paulo José's parents' house. As always, Renata helped her sister-in-law with the preparations, especially because Eunice was a little unwell, although she was very happy for her granddaughter's birthday.

– Everything is so beautiful!

Maria Helena was very grateful for everyone's efforts in making her birthday party happen. The more she grew, the kinder she became. Eunice liked to teach her granddaughters to paint, but since Esther did not have the same appreciation for painting, the grandmother had become much closer to Maria Helena.

On the day of the girl's birthday party Júlio received permission from his mentors to see how his daughter was doing. How happy Maria Helena was! All this helped him to improve himself and to evolve spiritually. The boy arrived with a bouquet of white flowers and placed them next to the portraits of Maria Helena and Eunice. Then he walked away.

***

Lourdes had received an Italian coat at the atelier to use as a model for a garment. When Marlene arrived to work, the two partners started talking. As soon as she saw the coat, she was instantly charmed.

– Lourdes! Whose beautiful coat is that?

– It was Mrs. Dirce who brought me to copy the model. She asked me to make a similar one in another color and with a different fabric.

Marlene began to feel unwell; she became dizzy and started to break into a cold sweat.

– Lourdes, I don't think I'm feeling very well. I wonder if you could get me some water.

– Of course. But what happened? You look pale! Has your blood pressure dropped? Did you eat properly?

– I don't know what's going on because I ate as usual. I feel very cold and I'm shivering.

Marlene then asked Lourdes to give her the coat that was in her hands. As soon as she touched it, the girl began to hear a voice asking her to look inside the pocket, because there was a velvet bag with some jewelry in it. The voice said:

"Keep this jewelry. There is a pair of earrings, a brooch, and a chain with a pendant."

Marlene repeated out loud what she had heard. That spirit was of an Italian woman who had lived in Brazil for fifty years and had disincarnated almost alone because she had only one nice, Tânia, who was married and rarely visited her. Rosa disincarnated at the age of 93 in her house and was found by her maid Norma. Tania took all her aunt's clothes to a thrift store and Mrs. Dirce ended up buying one of the deceased's coats.

– And now, Lourdes? What do I do?

– If it's a request from this woman and she told you all this, keep the jewelry. She was probably a good person.

– But don't you think we should give them to Mrs. Dirce, since she bought the coat? – asked Marlene, indecisively.

– I don't think so, because Mrs. Rosa came to talk to you.

– I will think about it and decide what to do.

That same night. Marlene had a dream in which she met Rosa. The woman was sitting in front of a house and told her that she had been the wife of a colonel, who passed away at the age of 80 and with whom she had no children. Again, the old woman said that she would like Marlene to keep the jewels because that would belong to her daughters when they grew up.

At dawn, Marlene could remember the dream, of Rosa's beautiful blue eyes and white hair. She could smell, even in a subtle way, the old woman's perfume.

Impressed, Marlene got up and quickly got ready for work. She had an urgent need to talk to her partner.

As soon as she arrived at the atelier Marlene told Lourdes that she would keep the jewelry without any conscience because she had met Rosa in a dream. The same day Marlene called Raul and told him what had happened and asked why her visions had increased.

– Raul, what is going on? Why is this happening more often?

These are your gifts, my friend. Your mediumship is opening. That's all very beautiful. I think the time has come for you to deal with this issue more seriously, no? What do you think about starting to work at Mrs. Mercedes' center?

– You're right. I think the moment has come. I'm ready!

Soon after, Marlene began to work at Mrs. Mercedes' center, developing her spirituality day by day.

After facing so many setbacks Marlene finally found the peace of mind, she so desperately sought with her great love Paulo José, her children Maria Helena, Ester and Carlinhos, and her family and friends. By trusting life and in her strength, she built her path.

EPILOGUE

Recently Renata started to wake up very tired and could not understand why.

One night during one of her exits from the body Renata saw herself near a house with several windows in which a man with a hat was walking. Behind the house was a crying girl with a cut on her leg that was bleeding profusely. She approached to try to help the girl, but soon a woman appeared holding a bundle of herbs wrapped in a cloth. The woman tied the ointment on the girl's cut.

– What happened to her?

The lady then told her that her husband was a very violent man and that her daughter had hurt herself trying to get away from him.

Renata bent down to place her hands on Livia's legs – as the girl was called – and began to tend to her cuts.

– You need to be very patient. Don't be afraid. Pray, for everything will pass.

The next morning, Renata got up and, after a few hours, ended up remembering the dream.

About ten days later, on another exit from the body, Renata finally had permission to meet Olavo. He was handsome and very well dressed.

– Give me your hands. Look! I'm fine now!

Renata, then, began to cry incessantly and asked him for forgiveness because she felt guilty for his death.

– Olavo, forgive me. My love was not enough to protect you.

In another life, Renata had been Luciana, a woman who married a very aggressive man and at a certain moment, no longer being able to stand the situation, abandoned him when she met Olavo, a man she fell in love with.

Luciana and Olavo began a romance, still on the sly, but the girl's husband found out about the betrayal and started to threaten her. Without caring about anything, the two continued to meet and Luciana became pregnant by Olavo. The girl's husband was sterile so, not knowing what to do, she told a maid who worked in the house about the child she was carrying in her womb. The woman, however, betrayed Luciana's trust and told everything to the boss who set an ambush for Olavo.

Together with some thugs he hired, the man beat Olavo severely and stabbed him to death. Luciana did not know what had happened to her lover because he had simply disappeared. She did not even have time to tell him about her pregnancy or to say goodbye to her lover.

Desperate, she began a frantic search for her beloved, but no one had seen him anywhere. After a few days they found Olavo's body in a bush. It was the boy's sister, Márcia, who helped Luciana to identify the body.

As soon as she saw her lover's body lying in the bushes Luciana fainted and only later, she told the police about her husband's threats. In time they ended up arresting all those involved in the murder.

– Márcia, I am pregnant with your brother's child, but I haven't even had time to tell him. How sad! How will I live without Olavo in my life?

– I will be with you to help raise this child, Luciana. Calm down.

And this really happened. Márcia was a teacher and as soon as the child was born, a beautiful girl named Dulce, the woman began to help Luciana raise the child. Dulce grew up to become a teacher and took care of her mother and aunt.

In the astral, Olavo went through a long period of healing and when he was already well, he approached Marcos because he already knew about the relationship that he and Renata would have. Olavo then became the protective spirit of both.

Renata had two children with Marcos, her great love, and continued to make her trips to the spiritual world because it was her way of working for spirituality. The apologies and farewells between Olavo and Renata helped a lot to fill the emptiness that existed inside her, even though the girl did not know the real reason for it.

Forgiving those who are already gone is an act that only the noble people can have. It is important to cultivate love and to believe in the power of life to achieve happiness.

The End..

Zibia Gasparetto's Greatest success stories

With more than 20 million titles sold, the author has contributed to the strengthening of spiritualist literature in the publishing market and to the popularization of spirituality. Learn more of the author's successes.

Romances Dictated by the Spirit Lucius

The Life Force

The Truth of each one

Life knows what it does

She trusted in life

Between Love and War

Esmeralda

Thorns of Time

Eternal Bonds

Nothing is by Chance

Nobody is Nobody's

God's Advocate

Tomorrow Belongs to God

Love Won

Unexpected Encounter

On the Edge of Destiny

The Sly One

The Morro of Illusions

Where is Teresa?

Through the Doors of the Heart
When Life chooses
When the Hour Comes
When it is necessary to return
Opening for Life
Not afraid to live
Only love can do it
We Are All Innocent
Everything has its price
It was all worth it
A real love
Overcoming the past

Other success stories by André Luiz Ruiz and Lucius
The Love Never Forgets You Trilogy
The Strength of Kindness
Under the Hands of Mercy
Saying Goodbye to Earth
At the End of the Last Hour
Sculpting Your Destiny
There are Flowers on the Stones
The Crags are made of Sand

Books of Eliana Machado Coelho and Schellida

Hearts without Destiny

The Shine of Truth

The Right to be Happy

The Return

In the Silence of Passions

Strength to Begin Again

The Certainty of Victory

The Conquest of Peace

Lessons Life Offers

Stronger than Ever

No Rules for Loving

A Diary in Time

A Reason to Live

Eliana Machado Coelho and Schellida, Romances that captivate, teach, move and can change your life!

Romances of Arandi Gomes Texeira and The Count J.W. Rochester

Lancaster County

The Power of Love

The Trial

Cleopatra's Bracelet

The Reincarnation of a Queen

You Are Gods

Books of Marcelo Cezar and Marco Aurelio

Love is for the Strong

The Last Chance

Nothing is as it Seems

Forever With Me

Only God Knows

You Make Tomorrow

A Breath of Tenderness

Books of Vera Kryzhanovskaia and JW Rochester

The Revenge of the Jew

The Nun of the Marriages

The Sorcerer's Daughter

The Flower of the Swamp

The Divine Wrath

The Legend of the Castle of Montignoso

The Death of the Planet

The Night of Saint Bartholomew

The Revenge of the Jew

Blessed are the poor in spirit

Cobra Capella

Dolores

Trilogy of the Kingdom of Shadows

From Heaven to Earth

Episodes from the Life of Tiberius

Infernal Spell

Herculanum

On the Frontier

Naema, the Witch

In the Castle of Scotland (Trilogy 2)

New Era

The Elixir of Long Life

The Pharaoh Mernephtah

The Lawgivers

The Magicians

The Terrible Phantom

Paradise without Adam

Romance of a Queen

Czech Luminaries

Hidden Narratives

The Nun of the Marriages

Books of Elisa Masselli

There is always a reason

Nothing goes unanswered

Life is made of decisions

The Mission of each one

Something more is needed

The Past does not matter

Destiny in his hands

God was with him

When the past does not pass

Just beginning

**Books of Vera Lúcia Marinzeck de Carvalhoç
and Patricia**

Violets in the Window

Living in the Spirit World

The Writer's House

Flight of the Seagull

**Vera Lúcia Marinzeck de Carvalho
and Antônio Carlos**

Love your Enemies

Slave Bernardino

the Rock of Lovers

Rosa, the third fatality

Captives and Freed

Books of Mónica de Castro y Leonel

In spite of everything

Love is not to be trifled with

Face to Face with the Truth

Of My Whole Being

I wish

The Price of Being Different

Twins

Giselle, The Inquisitor's Mistress

Greta

Till Life Do You Part

Impulses of the Heart

Jurema of the Jungle

The Actress

The Force of Destiny

Memories that the Wind Brings

Secrets of the Soul

Feeling in One's Own Skin

World Spiritist Institute

www.ingramcontent.com/pod-product-compliance
Lightning Source LLC
LaVergne TN
LVHW041223080526
838199LV00083B/2423